Building
Academic
Language
through Content-Area Text

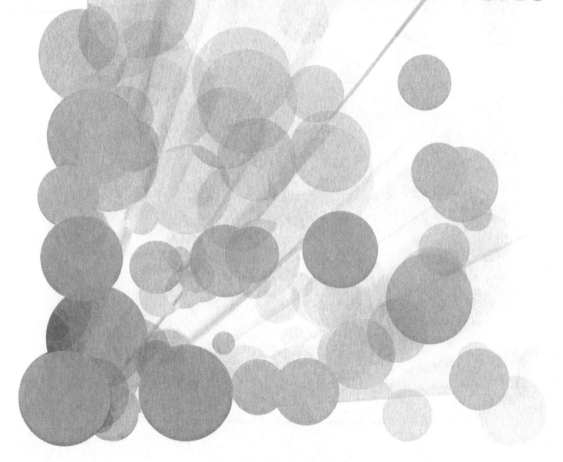

Authors

Erica R. Bowers, Ed.D.

Laura E. Keisler, Ed.D.

Contributing Author

Shanan Fitts, Ph.D.

SHELL EDUCATION

Publishing Credits

Dona Herweck Rice, *Editor-in-Chief*; Lee Aucoin, *Creative Director*;
Don Tran, *Print Production Manager;* Timothy J. Bradley, *Illustration Manager;*
Conni Medina, M.A.Ed., *Editorial Director;* Evelyn Garcia, *Associate Education Editor;*
Lisa Greathouse, *Contributing Editor;* Juan Chavolla, *Interior Layout Designer;*
Grace Alba, *Print Production;* Corinne Burton, M.A.Ed., *Publisher*

Shell Education
5301 Oceanus Drive
Huntington Beach, CA 92649-1030
http://www.shelleducation.com
ISBN 978-1-4258-0631-6
© 2011 by Shell Educational Publishing, Inc.

Table of Contents

Research

Academic language has become one of the hot topics in education over the past few years. When considering the tremendous increase in the number of English language learners in our classrooms, the role of academic language takes on even greater importance. The future of successfully educating English language learners will require teachers to support language acquisition every day in every classroom and during every lesson. By looking through the lens of academic language, we can design instruction that considers the language demands placed on English language learners and develop strategies that support language development in every area of learning, especially in the content areas. The goal of this book is to share those strategies and give you a road map for how to put them into action in your classroom.

What Is Academic Language?

Finding a clear, concise, common definition of the term *academic language* can prove elusive. Below are sample definitions found in literature:

- Academic language is "a variety or a register of English used in professional books and characterized by the specific linguistic features associated with academic disciplines" (Scarcella 2003, 19).

- "The difference between the 'everyday' and the 'specialist' lexis [words] is a major way that language of academic texts differs from the ordinary interactional language of daily life" (Schleppegrell 2004, 52).

- Academic language is language used to "access and engage with the school curriculum" (Bailey and Heritage 2008).

After spending much time researching, talking with educators, and seeing teachers use academic language strategies in the classroom, we have created the following definition:

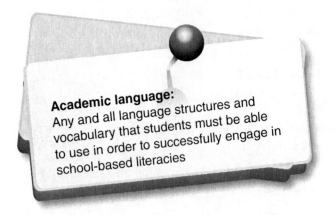

Academic language:
Any and all language structures and vocabulary that students must be able to use in order to successfully engage in school-based literacies

Academic language includes:

- both general and specific syntax and sentence structures.

- both general vocabulary and vocabulary specific to content areas.

By *success in school-based literacies,* we refer to:

- student literacy as it relates to specific content areas (e.g., mathematics, social studies, science).

- student literacy as it relates to literacy as a social construct (e.g., how well a student can negotiate the nuances of the cultures and values underlying the dominant language of school, in this case English).

Research *(cont.)*

The Changing Classroom

Teachers are facing the reality of an ever-growing number of students who speak a language other than English in the home. The following statistics bear this out:

- In 2000, 47 million people, or 18% of the population in the United States, spoke a language other than English at home. By 2030, this is projected to increase to 40%.

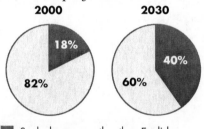

2000 **2030**

■ Spoke language other than English
□ Spoke English

- In 2006, approximately 10 million students in U.S. public schools spoke a language other than English in the home; 5.1 million of those students were classified as English language learners.

2006–10 Million Students Who Spoke a Language Other Than English at Home

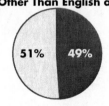

■ English Language Learners
□ Not English Language Learners

Additionally, in California public schools alone, 44.8% of students reported speaking a language other than English at home. Texas, New Mexico, and Arizona each report that more than 30% of their students speak a language other than English (U.S. Census Bureau 2006).

Are Teachers Prepared?

Federal and state governments have begun to pay serious attention to the progress of English language learners, but our schools remain unprepared for the exponential growth in the number of English language learners they will experience in less than 20 years. A sample of achievement data for English language learners paints a grim picture of their progress thus far. In 2007, only 30% of fourth-grade English language learners scored above basic proficiency in reading, compared with 70% of their English-speaking counterparts (National Center for Educational Statistics 2007). Scores were almost identical in fourth-grade math as well as eighth-grade reading and math.

Additionally, the National Center for Educational Statistics (NCES) reports that while 41% of teachers have been responsible for teaching English language learners in their classrooms, only about 13 percent have spent eight or more hours in professional development specific to teaching English language learners.

In the past, schools may have been able to accommodate the needs of English language learners by providing them with small-group interventions using an English as a Second Language (ESL) teacher or resource specialist. Indeed, in some districts not yet impacted by high numbers of English language learners, this still may be a viable solution—for now. But states like California and Texas, with over 500,000 English language learners each, paint a different picture of what serving these students will require (National Center for Educational Statistics 2006–2007). Pullout and resource support are no longer feasible options when English language learners compose half—or even 100%—of a classroom.

Research *(cont.)*

Why Teaching Academic Language Makes Sense for ELL Students

From the moment we are born, we begin to log countless hours learning our native language through our interactions with the world around us. Our brains catalog vocabulary, linguistic patterns, and speech registers; we cue in on the nuances of our language, turns of phrase, idiomatic expressions, and so on. We spend this time developing our proficiency and automaticity with our native language, which then supports our academic learning and future pursuits. When faced with learning a second language, the situation is different. Often, students are learning a new language and are required to learn all that native speakers have acquired in a much shorter period of time. Students are immersed in both the informal language of communicating with teachers and peers and in the formal language of the content areas they are being taught.

Students need to decode the meanings of the words their teachers are using during instruction, and often these words are describing big ideas or abstract concepts. Consider for a moment how challenging it can be for native English-speaking students to learn a topic like figurative language and then think about how difficult it might be to understand this concept in a second language! Compounding the challenge for English language learners is the fact that the time they have to learn English is often measured by hours spent in the classroom or on the playground. Many switch back to their native language at home and in their communities.

By focusing on academic language, we can design instruction that purposefully considers the language demands placed on English language learners and develop strategies and scaffolds that support language development in every area of learning, but especially in the content areas.

First Priority: Basic Oral Proficiency

For most students suddenly immersed into a new language in the classroom, the priority for both teacher and student will probably be on developing their ability to communicate with one another. Many English language learners achieve oral proficiency relatively quickly because of this need to communicate with those around them. Basic Interpersonal Communication Skills, or BICS—the everyday language of the classroom and the playground needed in social situations—begins to make sense as beginning speakers of English repeat and use the words they hear and receive support and feedback from their native English-speaking peers (Cummins 2003).

However, two pitfalls often present themselves as English language learners pass from the beginning to the intermediate stages of learning English.

The first pitfall concerns feedback. As soon as students are able to functionally communicate with their teachers and peers, the amount of effort they expend attending to English drops considerably (Scarcella 2003). In addition, as they begin to appear more confident in their use of the language, those around them begin to consider giving feedback on their use of English as rude or impolite. By receiving little to no feedback, English language learners receive the message that they are indeed competent communicators and therefore pay less and less attention to the words that they use and how they use them.

Research *(cont.)*

The second pitfall is a lack of accurate modeling. In order for students to build a strong foundation for the development of advanced academic literacy, it is important that immersion experiences are with fluent speakers of standard English. These fluent speakers should, in theory, be providing the learners with exposure to the correct phonology, lexicon, morphology, syntax, and pragmatics of the English language (Colombi and Schleppegrell 2002). However, many English language learners attend schools where the majority of students are English language learners themselves. Therefore, interactions and opportunities for practice of English (both inside and outside the classroom) occur not with speakers of standard English but rather with other learners of English who may not have acquired the accurate use of English necessary to build strong oral proficiency themselves (Wong-Fillmore and Snow 2000).

The research has shown that in these situations, one of two outcomes are likely:

- Students will not acquire advanced academic English without considerable intervention and end up making little progress in building their overall English proficiency.

- Students end up learning different forms of nonstandard English, which often differ greatly from the form of English necessary to develop advanced academic literacy (Wong-Fillmore and Snow 2000).

Obviously, neither outcome is desirable.

Goal: Academic Success

Simply by attending school, most English language learners will learn enough English to become proficient communicators, but without explicit teaching of academic language, they will be virtually shut out of the advanced academic language necessary for academic success. This level of language learning requires Cognitive Academic Language Proficiency, known as CALP, and includes listening, speaking, reading, and writing about subject-area content material (Cummins 2003). Every lesson should be seen as an opportunity to make these language demands explicit in our teaching and provide the interventions to support students' language needs.

Teachers also must be aware that oral proficiency can mask academic language deficiencies that may hinder overall academic achievement. Because English language learners are able to participate in discussions, ask questions, and engage in everyday language, it can be easy to overlook this gap between everyday language and academic language.

Further, while all teachers of English language learners need to be aware of this potential gap, it becomes even more critical as students progress from primary to intermediate and then to the secondary grades. For younger students, some of the discrepancy between proficiency in everyday and academic language may be mitigated by the explicit teaching they receive in a primary program—an emphasis on phonics, grammar, and basic features of text. For older students, the gap between everyday and academic language may continue to grow as less and less time is spent on explicit language instruction and emphasis on building content knowledge becomes paramount.

Academic Language and Literacy in the Content Areas

As teachers and as speakers of English, we know that there are many varieties of the English language. Each variety has a place and a purpose in our daily lives. For example, the way we speak at home with our families might be different from the way we speak in the classroom when we teach. We make choices about the variety of English we use based on the context of the situation.

This same notion of variety applies to English as a written language. The words and grammatical structures used to author a scientific lab report differ from the language used to write narrative fiction. A historian writing a biography of Abraham Lincoln is most likely going to use a variety of English much different than does an economist writing an article for a business journal. To speak or write the same variety of English in every context would be awkward in some situations and inappropriate in others.

Being able to communicate effectively from the playground to the science lab requires students to be proficient in many varieties of English, both the everyday and the academic.

Examination of the language used in different content areas reveals that each academic discipline has its own distinct register. Each register, or variety of language, includes both words used in the discipline and the ways in which language is constructed for meaning. Familiarity with differences in how language is used in each content area can go a long way in helping teachers support the English language learners in their classes.

Considerations for Teachers of English/Language Arts

As the focus of this content area is teaching literacy skills, it is easy to overlook the fact that English language arts also has discipline-specific vocabulary. In the context of learning these literacy skills, students encounter a great amount of terminology. Take for example a lesson on figurative language: *simile*, *metaphor*, and *idiom* are all specialized content words for literary devices that students need to learn, but think of how the word *like* is used in a simile. Students might need the teacher to be explicit about the fact that in this instance *like* is being used to mean "similar."

Equally as important is to consider the language demands being placed on English language learners as they practice literacy skills and strategies. When instructing on various comprehension skills and strategies, students will benefit from the use of graphic organizers, visuals, or mnemonics to associate with these skills. As students speak and write, providing resources such as discussion or writing prompts and sentence frames will help English language learners develop fluency in language arts as an academic discipline.

Academic Language and Literacy in the Content Areas *(cont.)*

Reading, Writing, and Speaking Like a Scientist

There has been much attention devoted to the study of academic language in the area of science. One possible reason for this focus is grounded in the logic of Wellington and Osborne (2001), who state that "learning the language of science is a major part (if not the major part) of science education." For example, consider this excerpt from a sixth-grade science text:

> When you initially get on your bicycle, it is stationary. Then, after you push on the pedals, the bicycle begins to move. This illustrates a simple fact—forces create changes in motion. The motion of an object is the result of all the forces acting on it. When the forces are equal or balanced, there is no change in motion; when the forces are unequal, there is a change in motion. If you don't continue pedaling, the bicycle slows down. The force that is acting on it is friction. Friction is the force that occurs when objects rub against each other. The tires of the bicycle rub against the pavement or sidewalk, causing friction, which eventually slows down the bicycle. You use friction to decrease the speed of the bicycle with your brakes.

In light of the text sample, it is no wonder why students struggle in their understanding of science for several reasons:

In science, language development and conceptual development are inextricably linked and, not surprisingly, students tend to confuse scientific concepts and vocabulary with everyday concepts and vocabulary. Wellington and Osborne determined that students' main problem seems to be more with everyday English words used in a science context (e.g., *mass, characteristic, consecutive,*

source) rather than with the specialized content vocabulary words. These everyday words tended to have multiple meanings that were not explicitly explained.

The format of science text differs from other text with which students are familiar. For example, an essential element of science is making hypotheses and explaining the rationale—in simpler terms, causes and effects. This uses logical connectives, which are essentially conjunctions used to join two or more simple sentences to imply a logic that joins them (e.g., If I add vinegar to the baking soda, then it will bubble.). In science, logical connectives can be used to form hypotheses, imply inferences, express comparisons and contrasts, and show causality.

Science textbooks require interpretation of "tables, charts, diagrams, graphs, maps, drawings, photographs, and a host of specialized visual representations" (Lemke 2002, 24). Students need to be able to "read" and interpret these modes of information and to communicate findings based upon them. Lemke emphasizes the importance of classroom dialogue, note taking, group work, application activities, textbook reading, report writing, and assessments for the development of scientific language.

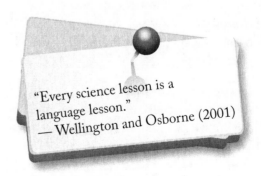

"Every science lesson is a language lesson."
— Wellington and Osborne (2001)

Academic Language and Literacy in the Content Areas *(cont.)*

Reading, Writing, and Speaking Like a Historian

Research has also focused on the distinct language, vocabulary, and organization used in social studies texts and teaching. Social studies texts typically use complex vocabulary and syntax, make undue assumptions regarding the background knowledge of the student, and fail to make explicit connections between historical events (Beck, McKeown, and Gromoll 1989; Schleppegrell, Achugar, and Oteíza 2004; Short 1994). For example, consider this excerpt from a fifth-grade social studies text:

> Huyana Kapac was the eleventh Incan emperor. He came to the throne in 1493. Under his rule, the empire grew. It reached its greatest power. The Incas now ruled all the land and people from Chile to what is now Colombia. Their empire was 2,500 miles (4,023.4 km) long.

Teaching literacy skills in the context of social studies is important for several reasons:

Social studies relies heavily on the textbook and teacher's lecture to present information (Short 1994).

Social studies demands high levels of literacy both in terms of comprehension and production of language. Students are expected to demonstrate their understanding of social studies in essays or reports.

Social studies texts employ a wide range of vocabulary and use words in unusual or unfamiliar ways. The sample text above uses idiomatic expressions *He came to the throne* and *Under his rule*, which can be confusing for English language learners.

Many discipline-specific vocabulary words found in social studies texts are generally not included in the glossary of the textbook and are difficult for students to define via context clues (Short 1994). Social studies texts include proper nouns that are linked to specific historical events (Bailey and Butler 2007; Marzano 2004) and nominalizations (changing a verb into a noun). They also represent the participants of historical events in abstract and depersonalized ways. For example, words such as *slavery* and *settlers* not only represent a concept or a group of people but also imply an interpretive framework, as well as a whole set of social and economic relations (Schleppegrell, Achugar, and Oteíza 2004).

Social studies texts utilize complex organizational features. These are fairly specific to historical narrative and combine characteristics of expository and narrative writing (Bailey and Butler 2007; Schleppegrell 2004). The first sentence is written like an expository or informational text, but the following two sentences take on a more narrative style before reverting back to expository at the end of the paragraph. Researchers have found that this organization was confusing for English language learners and relied upon the existence of prior knowledge that they simply did not possess.

Social studies texts typically incorporate many visuals that are meant to assist students in their interpretation of the text. These visuals include maps, charts, graphs, and time lines and are only helpful if time has been spent with students to make the organization of the text explicit and to build background knowledge on the topic being studied.

Academic Language and Literacy in the Content Areas *(cont.)*

Reading, Writing, and Speaking Like a Mathematician

Many teachers observe that their English language learners achieve at higher levels in mathematics than in other content areas. They then conclude that math is relatively free of language demands, unlike science and social studies. However, research has demonstrated that math is actually a language of highly specialized vocabulary that students are unlikely to encounter in everyday, more informal conversation, or reading (Chamot and O'Malley 1996). For example, consider this text taken from a second-grade mathematics text:

> Patterns can be found everywhere—in numbers and in shapes, for example. So, it is not surprising that the strategy of "Looking for a Pattern" is used often.
>
> When you find a pattern, it becomes easy to predict what comes next.
>
> You may use more than one strategy to solve a problem. As you learn more about "Looking for a Pattern," you will find that drawing a table is often the best way to see a pattern.

Take a look at the sample text. There are numerous academic vocabulary words such as *pattern*, *shapes*, and *strategy* that may be unfamiliar to English language learners.

In order to be successful, students need to know the meanings of discipline-specific words such as *pattern* or *shapes* but also be aware that more familiar words such as *table* take on new meanings in mathematics (Cuevas 1984). The ways in which even the most familiar of words might be used differently in math poses a potential problem for English language learners.

In addition to the vocabulary students must comprehend, analysis of the math register reveals five common syntactic features (Spanos, Rhodes, Dale, and Crandall 1988). Math relies heavily on the use of the following:

- comparatives (greater than/less than)

- prepositions (divided by)

- the passive voice (*x* is defined as)

- reversals (*a* is five less than *b*)

- logical connectives (if_____, then _____)

Proficiency Levels for English Language Learners

All teachers should know the levels of language proficiency for each of their English language learners. Knowing these levels will help to plan instruction. (The category titles and numbers of levels vary from district to district or state to state, but the general descriptions are common.) Students at level 1 will need a lot of language support during instruction. Using visuals to support oral and written language will help make the language more comprehensible. These students "often understand much more than they are able to express" (Herrell and Jordan 2004). It is the teacher's job to move them from just listening to language to expressing language. Students at levels 2 and 3 will benefit from pair work in speaking tasks, but they will need

additional individual support during writing and reading tasks. Students at levels 4 and 5 (or 6, in some cases) may appear to be fully proficient in the English language. However, because they are English language learners, they may still struggle with comprehending the academic language used during instruction. They may also struggle with reading and writing.

The following chart shows the proficiency levels for English language learners at a quick glance. These proficiency levels are based on the World-Class Instructional Design and Assessment (WIDA) Consortium (WIDA 2007).

Proficiency Levels at a Quick Glance

Proficiency Level	Questions to Ask	Activities/Actions		
Level 1— Beginning (Entering) minimal comprehension no verbal production	Where is…? What is the main idea? What examples do you see? What are the parts of…? Which was your favorite…? What would be different if…?	listen	draw	mime
		point	circle	respond (with one or two words)
Level 2— Early Intermediate (Beginning) limited comprehension short spoken phrases	Can you list three…? Tell me. What facts or ideas show…? When will you use…? How is…related to…? What is your opinion of…? What way would you design…?	move	select	act/act out
		match	choose	list

Proficiency Levels for English Language Learners *(cont.)*

Proficiency Level	Questions to Ask	Activities/Actions		
Level 3—Intermediate (Developing) increased comprehension simple sentences	How did…happen? Which is the best answer…? What do you already know about…? Why do you think…? How would you evaluate…? What would happen if…?	name	list	respond (with phrases or sentences)
		label	categorize	paraphrase
		tell/say	analyze	justify
Level 4—Early Advanced (Expanding) very good comprehension some errors in speech	How would you show…? How would you summarize…? What would result if…? What is the relationship between…? Would it be better if…? What is an alternative…?	recall	retell	define
		compare/contrast	explain	restate
		describe	role-play	create
Level 5—Advanced (Bridging) comprehension comparable to native-English speakers speaks using complex sentences	What were the most obvious…? What is true about…? How would you use…? What ideas justify…? How would you have advised…? How would you improve…?	analyze	defend	complete
		evaluate	justify	support
		create	describe	express

How to Use This Book

Building Academic Language through Content-Area Text: Strategies to Support English Language Learners shows teachers how to plan content-area lessons in order to support the development of academic language.

This book is designed around a practical planning template that will help teachers plan effective content-area lessons that support academic language. There are four main sections: Planning for Explicit Teaching, Schema and Vocabulary Building, Comprehensible Input, and Opportunities for Practice.

Planning for Explicit Teaching

This section guides teachers in analyzing any content-area text for key vocabulary and unfamiliar language.

Planning for Explicit Teaching			
Vocabulary			Language
Specialized Content:	General Academic:	Everyday:	Features: Functions:
Strategies			
Schema and Vocabulary Building:	Comprehensible Input:		Opportunities for Practice:

Schema and Vocabulary Building

This section provides teachers with the strategies they need to help increase students' understanding and retention of content by connecting the new content to pre-existing or prior knowledge.

Comprehensible Input

This section offers strategies for breaking down the delivery of input (information) in smaller, more manageable chunks for students to be able to easily understand the content.

Opportunities for Practice

This section features several active participation strategies that will help guide students in practicing the language skills they are learning.

How to Use This Book (cont.)

Each of the four main sections (Planning for Explicit Teaching, Schema and Vocabulary Building, Comprehensible Input, and Opportunities for Practice) includes strategies that implement the latest research in effective academic language instruction along with examples specific to language arts, mathematics, science, and social studies that represent real classroom applications.

The **Overview** gives a quick summary of the strategy.

McREL and TESOL Standards are listed for each strategy.

Directions are provided for each activity to let you know exactly how the strategy should flow.

Each strategy has three grade span examples that show how the strategy can be integrated into a content-area lesson to build both content knowledge and academic language.

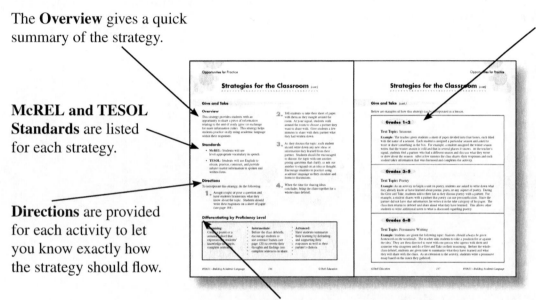

Each strategy includes a **Differentiating by Proficiency Level** section that provides suggestions for meeting the needs of students at the beginning, intermediate, and advanced language proficiency levels. Additionally, see pages 12–13 for proficiency levels at a quick glance.

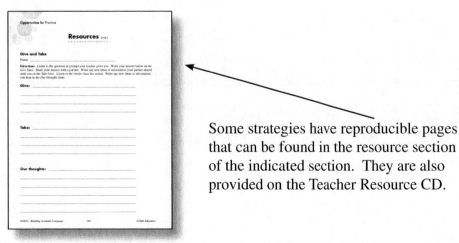

Some strategies have reproducible pages that can be found in the resource section of the indicated section. They are also provided on the Teacher Resource CD.

How to Use This Book (cont.)

● ●

The Lesson Design section starting on page 167 shows teachers how the strategies presented throughout the book can be incorporated into the template to support English language learners by emphasizing academic language. Additionally, this section will review each quadrant of the template to reassure that teachers are planning for explicit teaching.

At the end of the Lesson Design section are completed lesson design templates and sample lessons that bring together the strategies explored in the previous sections. There are three completed lessons: grades 1–2 (language arts), 3–5 (mathematics), and 6–8 (science), each of which includes the essential elements of effective instruction.

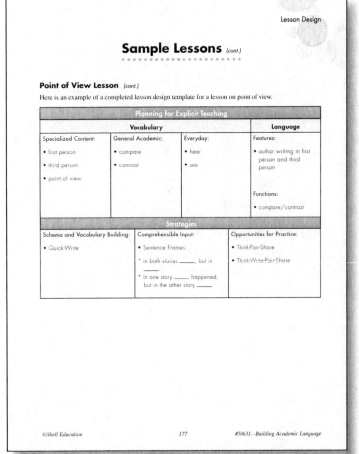

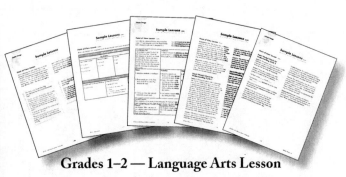

Grades 1–2 — Language Arts Lesson

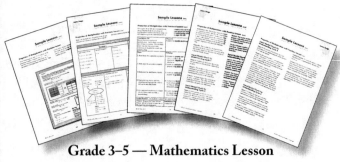

Grade 3–5 — Mathematics Lesson

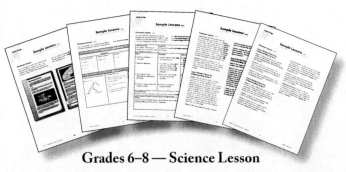

Grades 6–8 — Science Lesson

Introduction to Correlations

Shell Educational Publishing is committed to producing educational materials that are research and standards-based. In this effort we have correlated all of our products to the academic standards of all 50 states, the District of Columbia, and the Department of Defense Dependent Schools, as well as to the Common Core Standards.

Purpose and Intent of Standards

The No Child Left Behind legislation mandates that all states adopt academic standards that identify the skills students will learn in kindergarten through grade twelve. While many states had already adopted academic standards prior to NCLB, the legislation set requirements to ensure that the standards were detailed and comprehensive.

Standards are designed to focus instruction and guide adoption of curricula. Standards are statements that describe the criteria necessary for students to meet specific academic goals. They define the knowledge, skills, and content students should acquire at each level. Standards are also used to develop standardized tests to evaluate students' academic progress.

In many states today, teachers are required to demonstrate how their lessons meet state standards. State standards are used in development of all of our products, so educators can be assured they meet the academic requirements of each state. Complete standards correlation reports for each state can be printed directly from our website as well.

How to Find Standards Correlations

To print a correlation report for this product, visit our website at **http://www.seppub.com** and follow the on-screen directions. If you require assistance in printing correlation reports, please contact Customer Service at 1-877-777-3450.

McREL Compendium We use the Mid-continent Research for Education and Learning (McREL) Compendium to create standards correlations. Each year, McREL analyzes state standards and revises the compendium. By following this procedure, McREL is able to produce a general compilation of national standards. Each lesson in this product is based on one or more McREL standards. The chart on the following page lists each standard taught in this product and the page numbers for the corresponding lessons.

TESOL Standards

The lessons in this book promote English language development for English language learners. The standards listed on page 18, from the Teachers of English to Speakers of Other Languages (TESOL) Association, support the language objectives presented throughout the lessons.

Correlation to Standards

The main focus of the strategies presented in *Building Academic Language through Content-Area Text: Strategies to Support English Language Learners* is to promote the development of academic language. The chart below lists the standards correlated to the strategies included in this book.

McREL Compendium Language Arts Standards	Page
1.5—Uses strategies to organize written work	54, 58, 62
5.3—Uses a variety of strategies to extend reading vocabulary	66, 70, 74, 78, 82
5.4—Uses specific strategies to clear up confusing parts of a text	86
5.6—Understands level-appropriate sight words and vocabulary	120
5.7—Understands level-appropriate reading vocabulary	118
8.2—Asks and responds to questions about the meaning of words	114, 116
8.5—Uses level-appropriate vocabulary in speech	44, 46, 48, 50, 110, 112, 136, 138, 140, 142, 144, 146, 148, 150, 152, 154, 156, 158
TESOL Standards	**Page**
1.3—To use English to communicate in social settings: Students will use learning strategies to extend their communicative competence	142, 144
2.2—To use English to achieve academically in all content areas: Students will use English to obtain, process, construct, and provide subject matter information in spoken and written form	44, 46, 48, 50, 54, 58, 62, 66, 70, 74, 78, 82, 86, 120, 136, 138, 140, 146, 148, 150, 152, 154, 156, 158
2.3—To use English to achieve academically in all content areas: Students will use appropriate learning strategies to construct and apply academic knowledge	110, 112, 114, 116, 118

Planning for Explicit Teaching

Planning for Explicit Teaching			
Vocabulary			**Language**
Specialized Content:	General Academic:	Everyday:	Features:
			Functions:
Strategies			
Schema and Vocabulary Building:	Comprehensible Input:	Opportunities for Practice:	

Being Explicit

What Is Explicit Teaching of Academic Language?

Explicit teaching: Providing purposeful, systematic, and direct instruction of the features and functions of the English language during content-area instruction

In general, explicit teaching refers to carefully planned, often highly structured instruction. We can think of it as the opposite of *embedded* or implicit teaching of concepts, skills, or strategies.

Explicit teaching is a "let me tell you upfront" approach to instruction. Teachers identify potential stumbling blocks to student learning and understanding and use explicit teaching strategies to point out these potential problems during the course of instruction.

When applied to academic language, teachers are identifying elements of the English language that might pose a problem for English language learners and would interfere with their understanding of the content being taught. Specifically, explicit teaching requires delivering highly structured input to students on the meaning of both general and specific vocabulary, instruction on the grammatical and syntactical features of language used in texts, and teaching the cognitive functions of language.

Explicit teaching also includes teacher modeling, demonstration, or explanation of the concept(s) and/or words being taught. Often teachers will stop throughout their teaching of the lesson to highlight important concepts, to "think-aloud" or otherwise make explicit exactly what students should focus their attention on. Instruction is generally followed by guided practice in which students have the opportunity to practice what they have just learned, while the teacher or peers are made available to help.

Why Should Teachers Be Explicit About Academic Language?

When students encounter academic text, they face many challenges. They must create meaning of language containing unfamiliar vocabulary, of familiar words whose meaning may be context dependent, of complex grammatical combinations of words, of confusing or complicated sentence structures, or perhaps of figurative and idiomatic language that defies literal interpretation. While English language learners are particularly in need of support in pointing out these words, features, and expressions to gain a deeper understanding of the text, doing so benefits all students in the classroom.

Being Explicit (cont.)

Why Should Teachers Be Explicit About Academic Language? (cont.)

Teachers plan for their lessons in many different ways. Some write detailed lesson plans for each lesson they teach, while others simply list the objectives they wish for students to meet. Whichever your individual style, incorporating a focus on teaching academic language requires some additional planning. We call this planning through the "lens of academic language." Wearing this "lens" means looking at your curriculum and the content you teach through the eyes of an English language learner. We will address sample lesson design specifics later in the book. However, regardless of your lesson design, below are some of the questions a teacher might begin to consider when planning an outline for explicit teaching of academic language during the lessons of the unit or theme.

- What is the **specialized content vocabulary** that might be unfamiliar to students?

- What **general academic vocabulary** might students need in order to comprehend the text and generate quality written and oral responses during the lesson?

- Is **everyday vocabulary** used in an unfamiliar way in the text (e.g., are there words with multiple meanings that need to be identified for students)?

- Are there other **linguistic features** of text specific to this genre that need to be identified for students (e.g., sentence structure, voice, grammatical features)?

- Which **cognitive functions** of language are used in the text (e.g., will students be expected to compare and contrast, recognize cause and effect, classify and categorize)?

Explicit teaching happens when teachers ask themselves these questions and devote instructional time to directly teaching the answers. Explicit teaching of academic language also allows students to be aware of types of words and features of language that are specific to the content area they are studying as the teacher brings them to light. They are learning the language of an academic discipline. Note that the five aspects of academic language are included in the Planning for Explicit Teaching section of the lesson design template shown below.

Planning for Explicit Teaching			
Vocabulary			Language
Specialized Content:	General Academic:	Everyday:	Features: Functions:
Strategies			
Schema and Vocabulary Building:	Comprehensible Input:		Opportunities for Practice:

Elements of Academic Language

Functions of Language

Developing academic language proficiency requires students to explain, analyze, and evaluate text. Specifically, content-area text can require students to compare and contrast, classify and categorize, sequence, summarize, recognize cause and effect, and determine fact and opinion.

Take a look at the following science sample text below.

> Both alligators and crocodiles have an exceptionally long fourth tooth on either side of the lower jaw. When the alligator closes its mouth, these teeth slip into an open space in the upper jaw and seem to disappear. However, when the crocodile's mouth closes, these teeth protrude from the upper jaw, remaining visible.

An academically literate reader should immediately recognize that the purpose of this reading is comparing and contrasting alligators and crocodiles. There are words that signal this function of language in this passage. The word *both* signals to the reader a feature the reptiles share, while the word *however* signals a difference in characteristics.

The student recognizing this feature of the text has a tremendous advantage in terms of learning. The recognition of the compare-and-contrast organization gives the student a way to start processing the information and to ask himself or herself questions about the reading. After reading this passage, a student may automatically ask a question such as "Which reptile's tooth disappears?" Going back to quickly scan the text to answer that question aids in information processing, and the student starts to organize the information.

The student who does not recognize the compare-and-contrast organization is perhaps reading the passage sentence by sentence. In not recognizing that the information in each sentence should be read in comparison to the previous sentences, he or she may struggle to organize the information and ultimately not fully comprehend all the important parts of the passage.

Some examples of comprehension strategies within the functions of language include:

- cause and effect
- compare and contrast
- classify and categorize
- fact and opinion
- sequence
- summarize

Elements of Academic Language *(cont.)*

Explicitly Teaching Functions of Language

In thinking about how a teacher might explicitly teach students to attend to the functions of language as they read, consider the comprehension strategy of *compare and contrast*. Students should be aware that words and phrases such as *like, similarly, still, likewise, in comparison to, at the same time as,* and *in the same manner* all signal that a comparison is being made, while words and phrases such as *however, but, yet, nevertheless, nonetheless, conversely, rather, on the other hand,* and *on the contrary* signal a contrast. Often our focus is on the particular lesson topic; however, including attention to function may go great lengths in helping students master the new content. In this case, knowing these signal words gives them a cognitive framework for analyzing text as they read. (See pages 125–126 for sample signal words.)

Features of Language

Features of language include grammatical features, sentence structure, and vocabulary. Often, instruction on grammar and sentence structure is reserved for language arts instruction. However, the grammatical features of content-area text are often quite complex. In order for students to deconstruct text, they need knowledge of the correct usage of these complex grammatical features.

As an example of the complex features of language often used in social studies texts, look at the following excerpt about Genghis Khan.

> As a boy, Temujin was captured by a rival tribe. He escaped slavery and lived as an outlaw. He was not especially strong, and he never learned to read. Yet he and his children conquered much of the known world. At its height, their empire stretched from China west to the edge of Europe. To the south, it stretched into most of the Middle East and parts of India.

The underlying cues given by the language used in this passage are critical to understanding its meaning. Consider the features of language that students must know to fully interpret this text.

- Adding *-ed* at the ends of verbs such as *escape, live,* and *conquer* and the use of the word *was* should signal to the reader that he or she is reading about something that has happened in the past.

- The phrases *As a boy* and *Yet he and his children* are important temporal frames of reference that are used by a reader to locate time and sequence in a passage.

- The phrase *To the south, it stretched…* is yet another temporal frame of reference used to describe the location and size of the Mongol empire—both concepts important to understanding the topic.

- *At its height…* is an example of an idiomatic expression whose meaning might be lost by a student who is reading the statement literally, unaware of the concepts or ideas implied by this commonly used phrase.

This example presents a compelling argument for the teaching of language skills during content-area instruction.

Elements of Academic Language *(cont.)*

Vocabulary

Identifying academic vocabulary and teaching it explicitly is a key feature in supporting advanced academic literacy. Content-area instruction is rich with vocabulary. Students encounter many unfamiliar words and are often required to learn lists of words specific to the topic of study.

When thinking about teaching academic language, we shift our vocabulary focus from a concentration on content vocabulary to a mixed approach. This mixed approach combines the learning of specialized content vocabulary essential to understanding the topic with general academic words that students are likely to encounter in many subject areas and whose meaning is dependent upon the context. Students may be familiar with these words but find that they may be used in unfamiliar or unique ways in a particular content area. When looking through the lens of academic language, we can think about the vocabulary words and how we want to teach them based on the following classifications: specialized content, general academic, and everyday.

Specialized Content Vocabulary

Specialized content vocabulary are the words or terms that are content specific. Students need these words to build and expand their understanding of concepts related to the content.

In any content area, these are the words that are critical to understanding the topic under study. In addition to providing a rich exposure to these words and establishing a word-conscious environment, teachers should provide direct instruction of the specialized content vocabulary.

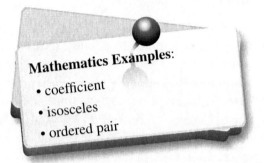

Mathematics Examples:
- coefficient
- isosceles
- ordered pair

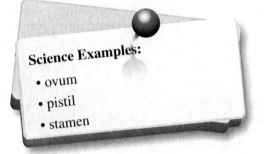

Science Examples:
- ovum
- pistil
- stamen

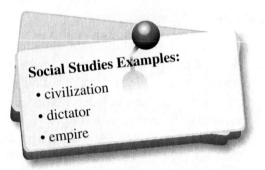

Social Studies Examples:
- civilization
- dictator
- empire

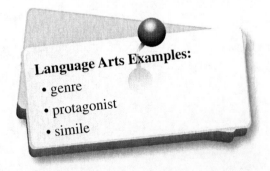

Language Arts Examples:
- genre
- protagonist
- simile

Elements of Academic Language (cont.)

General Academic Vocabulary

These are the words that some might consider to be the "language of school." These are words students are likely to encounter in written text, such as textbooks, and should be words they adapt into their own vocabulary, written and oral, as they become more academically literate. These words are not specific to any discipline but are used across content areas. Many of these words will be repeated over and over again during the lessons, so it may not be important to spend a lot of instructional time on them in every lesson; rather, build their use into lessons and design opportunities for students to practice them over and over again in different lessons. Students need to know how to use these words in order to comprehend content-area text and produce their own academic writing and speaking.

General Academic Vocabulary Examples:

- advantage
- category
- fact
- familiar
- opinion
- progress
- propose
- research
- review
- write

Elements of Academic Language (cont.)

Everyday Vocabulary

Everyday vocabulary includes words that have multiple meanings; they can take on very different meanings in a particular content area than they do as a part of a student's everyday oral and written vocabulary. As mentioned previously, it is often these words, as opposed to the specialized content vocabulary, that can interfere with student understanding (Wellington and Osborne 2001). We can find a common example of this issue in mathematics. Look at the sample below.

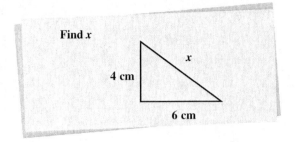

The word *find* is a very common word and one with which most students should be familiar. But consider an English language learner using his or her knowledge of everyday vocabulary to answer this problem. The prompt tells them to "find x." What if they put a circle around the x and then went on to the next problem? By most definitions of the word *find*, they have completed the task! Of course, as teachers, we are aware that in this context, *find* does not mean to locate the letter x but to *solve* for x. Students may need to be explicitly taught the meaning of *find* in the context of mathematics.

To see that this does not just occur in mathematics, look at the sentences below, taken from a passage on weather in a science text.

> ...all weather happens in the layer of atmosphere closest to Earth's surface. Many things affect weather. The biggest factors are heat, water, and wind.

In order to be successful in their study of weather, students need to know the specialized content vocabulary of the unit, such as the word *atmosphere*. This word is a logical choice for inclusion in the content-specific vocabulary that students should learn. But what about more common words students may need to study? English language learners in the class might need instruction on the word *affect*, particularly in distinguishing it from the word *effect*. Additionally, instruction on the meaning of *factors* could be beneficial. *Factor* is a word students likely learned in mathematics, and while its general meaning is similar to its use in science, explicit teaching of this word would help any student struggling to make that link.

Below is an example from a social studies passage.

> The Civil Rights Movement brought attention to the importance of the First Amendment Rights.

Again, students need to know the specialized content vocabulary such as *Civil Rights Movement*, but a word such as *attention* is classified as *everyday* vocabulary because this word can have another meaning in a student's everyday oral and written vocabulary.

Analyzing Content-Area Text

The beginning of this section focused on the key aspects of the development of academic language: functions of language, features of language, and vocabulary. The three content-area examples on the following pages show how to look at a piece of content-area text through the lens of academic language and identify the language to include in a lesson.

Planning for Explicit Teaching			
Vocabulary			**Language**
Specialized Content:	**General Academic:**	**Everyday:**	**Features:**
Is there specialized vocabulary that might be unfamiliar to students? (e.g., *stamen*, *pistil*)	What general academic vocabulary might students need to comprehend the text and generate quality written and oral responses during the lesson? (e.g., *analyze*, *infer*)	Are there everyday words in the text that are used in an unfamiliar way? (e.g., *table*)	Are there linguistic features of text specific to this genre that need to be identified for students (e.g., sentence structure, voice, grammatical features)? **Functions:** Which cognitive functions will be required to comprehend the text (e.g., compare and contrast, cause and effect, sequence)?

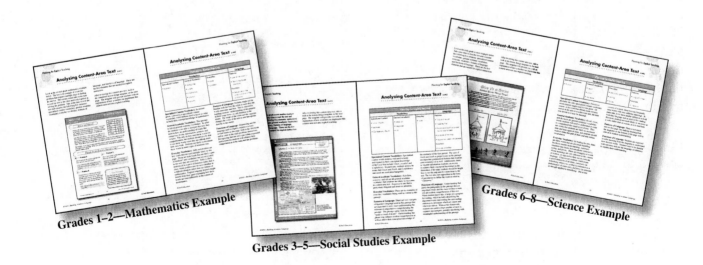

Grades 1–2—Mathematics Example

Grades 3–5—Social Studies Example

Grades 6–8—Science Example

Analyzing Content-Area Text (cont.)

Look at the second-grade mathematics example below. The text is an example of a real-life problem that requires multiple steps in finding the answer. The teacher would take some time to read the text to the class and work together in solving the problem. Take some time to read the text and consider the following five elements: specialized content vocabulary, general academic vocabulary, everyday vocabulary, features of

language, and functions of language. These are the five elements of academic language.

After reviewing this content-area text, look at the completed lesson design template on the next page. The template shows how this text can be analyzed in preparation for explicit teaching of academic language.

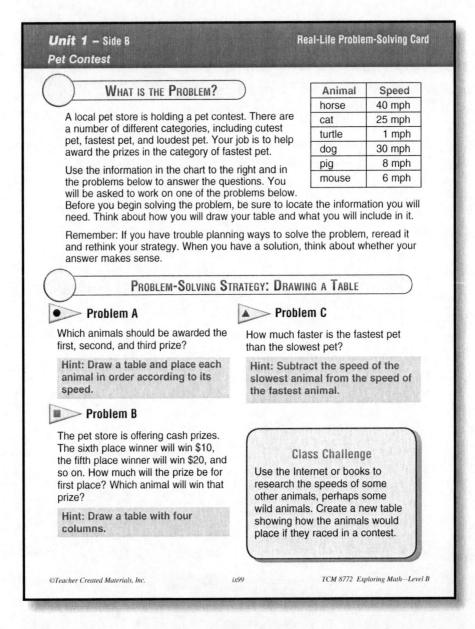

Unit 1 – Side B
Pet Contest

Real-Life Problem-Solving Card

WHAT IS THE PROBLEM?

A local pet store is holding a pet contest. There are a number of different categories, including cutest pet, fastest pet, and loudest pet. Your job is to help award the prizes in the category of fastest pet.

Use the information in the chart to the right and in the problems below to answer the questions. You will be asked to work on one of the problems below.
Before you begin solving the problem, be sure to locate the information you will need. Think about how you will draw your table and what you will include in it.

Remember: If you have trouble planning ways to solve the problem, reread it and rethink your strategy. When you have a solution, think about whether your answer makes sense.

Animal	Speed
horse	40 mph
cat	25 mph
turtle	1 mph
dog	30 mph
pig	8 mph
mouse	6 mph

PROBLEM-SOLVING STRATEGY: DRAWING A TABLE

Problem A

Which animals should be awarded the first, second, and third prize?

Hint: Draw a table and place each animal in order according to its speed.

Problem B

The pet store is offering cash prizes. The sixth place winner will win $10, the fifth place winner will win $20, and so on. How much will the prize be for first place? Which animal will win that prize?

Hint: Draw a table with four columns.

Problem C

How much faster is the fastest pet than the slowest pet?

Hint: Subtract the speed of the slowest animal from the speed of the fastest animal.

Class Challenge

Use the Internet or books to research the speeds of some other animals, perhaps some wild animals. Create a new table showing how the animals would place if they raced in a contest.

©Teacher Created Materials, Inc.   ix99   TCM 8772 Exploring Math—Level B

Analyzing Content-Area Text *(cont.)*

Planning for Explicit Teaching			
Vocabulary			**Language**
Specialized Content:	General Academic:	Everyday:	Features:
• subtract	• categories	• table	• Use of the colon (:)
	• locate	• problem	• Text in the boxes (captions)
	• information		Functions:
	• solution		• Sequence (in the directions and in the problems)
	• column		

Specialized Content Vocabulary: In second grade, *subtract* is a specialized content vocabulary word students need to know in order to build their concept knowledge in mathematics.

General Academic Vocabulary: This passage is full of general academic vocabulary. In order for students to be able to interpret this text, they need to have an understanding of words like *categories*, *locate*, *information*, *solution*, and *column*. Not only do they need these words for comprehension, but students should also be able to use these words when they are talking about their own work. Students are likely to encounter these words in many types of academic text.

Everyday Vocabulary: *Table* and *problem* are key words that are used multiple times on this page. These are both words that are likely a part of students' oral vocabulary but not necessarily in the way they are used here. *Table* is likely understood as a piece of furniture rather than a chart, while *problem* may be more familiar as a difficult situation rather than an element of mathematics. English language learners might benefit from time spent explaining how these words are used differently in the context of mathematics.

Features of Language: Students might not be familiar with the way the colon is used after the words *remember* and *hint*. This is critical for building students' understanding of the purpose of their usage here—to call attention to the reader. The usage of the colon and the captions changes the voice of the text to one that speaks directly to the reader.

Functions of Language: Sequencing and the language used to express sequence is used several times on this page, both in the directions and in some of the math problems themselves. Recognizing that the text is providing sequential instructions for students will enhance their comprehension of the tasks and the problems.

Analyzing Content-Area Text *(cont.)*

Look at the fifth-grade social studies example below. Take some time to read the text and consider the following five elements: specialized content vocabulary, general academic vocabulary, everyday vocabulary, features of language, and functions of language. These are the five elements of academic language.

After reviewing this content-area text, take a look at the lesson design template on the next page. The template shows how this text can be analyzed in preparation for explicit teaching of academic language.

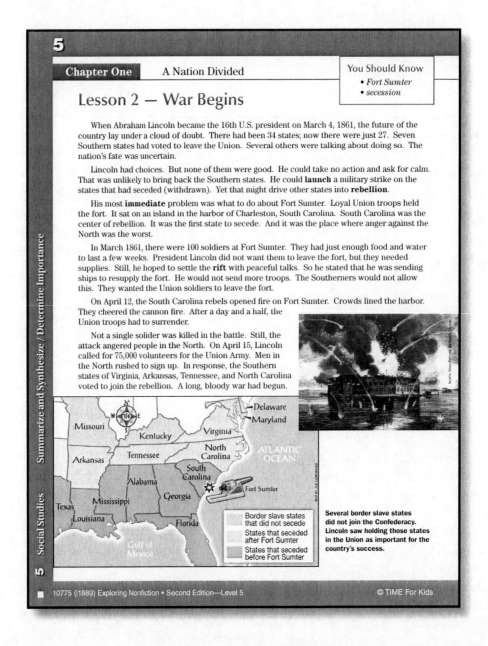

5

| Chapter One | A Nation Divided |

You Should Know
• *Fort Sumter*
• secession

Lesson 2 — War Begins

When Abraham Lincoln became the 16th U.S. president on March 4, 1861, the future of the country lay under a cloud of doubt. There had been 34 states; now there were just 27. Seven Southern states had voted to leave the Union. Several others were talking about doing so. The nation's fate was uncertain.

Lincoln had choices. But none of them were good. He could take no action and ask for calm. That was unlikely to bring back the Southern states. He could **launch** a military strike on the states that had seceded (withdrawn). Yet that might drive other states into **rebellion**.

His most **immediate** problem was what to do about Fort Sumter. Loyal Union troops held the fort. It sat on an island in the harbor of Charleston, South Carolina. South Carolina was the center of rebellion. It was the first state to secede. And it was the place where anger against the North was the worst.

In March 1861, there were 100 soldiers at Fort Sumter. They had just enough food and water to last a few weeks. President Lincoln did not want them to leave the fort, but they needed supplies. Still, he hoped to settle the **rift** with peaceful talks. So he stated that he was sending ships to resupply the fort. He would not send more troops. The Southerners would not allow this. They wanted the Union soldiers to leave the fort.

On April 12, the South Carolina rebels opened fire on Fort Sumter. Crowds lined the harbor. They cheered the cannon fire. After a day and a half, the Union troops had to surrender.

Not a single solider was killed in the battle. Still, the attack angered people in the North. On April 15, Lincoln called for 75,000 volunteers for the Union Army. Men in the North rushed to sign up. In response, the Southern states of Virginia, Arkansas, Tennessee, and North Carolina voted to join the rebellion. A long, bloody war had begun.

Several border slave states did not join the Confederacy. Lincoln saw holding those states in the Union as important for the country's success.

Border slave states that did not secede
States that seceded after Fort Sumter
States that seceded before Fort Sumter

Summarize and Synthesize / Determine Importance

Social Studies

5

10775 (i1989) Exploring Nonfiction • Second Edition—Level 5   © TIME For Kids

Analyzing Content-Area Text *(cont.)*

Planning for Explicit Teaching			
Vocabulary			**Language**
Specialized Content:	General Academic:	Everyday:	Features:
• Union (North) • seceded • Confederacy (South)	• rebellion • response • rift	• held	• "cloud of doubt" • "opened fire" • North and South as proper nouns (capitalized) • purpose of the map • apposition used with *secede* Functions: • cause and effect

Specialized Content Vocabulary: Specialized content words students will need to build and expand on their conceptual knowledge of the Civil War include *Union, seceded,* and *Confederacy.* In particular, students need to be aware that *Union* and *North,* and *Confederacy* and *South* are used interchangeably.

General Academic Vocabulary: *Rebellion, response,* and *rift* are all general academic vocabulary that students are likely to encounter in content-area text. *Response* is one that is particularly frequent and deserves attention.

Everyday Vocabulary: The word *held* is an example of a word that is likely a part of students' oral vocabulary. Students should understand that the word is used differently in this context.

Features of Language: There are two examples of figurative language used in this passage that are important to note, since understanding the reference is important to comprehending the passage. The passage opens with the image "under a cloud of doubt." Understanding this phrase will enhance student comprehension as well as add to their conceptual knowledge of the sentiment of the time period. The uses of *North* and *South* as proper nouns in the passage are important grammatical features that students need awareness of as well. Additionally, there is valuable information students can access to enhance their conceptual knowledge in the illustration of the map; students should be taught how to use the map and its connections to the text. The text also uses apposition in the form of parentheses to define the word *seceded* as "withdrawn."

Functions of Language: Understanding that particular paragraphs in this passage discuss important events and the causes of these events will aid student comprehension of this text. When students know this, it helps set a purpose for reading, which includes identifying the important events and reading the surrounding sentences to determine which are causes and which are effects. Without this framework, students encounter a large number of facts to organize and interpret, possibly interfering with meaningful understanding of the passage.

Analyzing Content-Area Text (cont.)

Look at the sixth-grade science example below. Take some time to read the text and consider the following five elements: specialized content vocabulary, general academic vocabulary, everyday vocabulary, features of language, and functions of language. These are the five elements that are needed for explicit instruction.

After reviewing this content-area text, take a look at the lesson design template on the next page. The template will provide you with an explanation of how a teacher can implement this content-area text into explicit teaching.

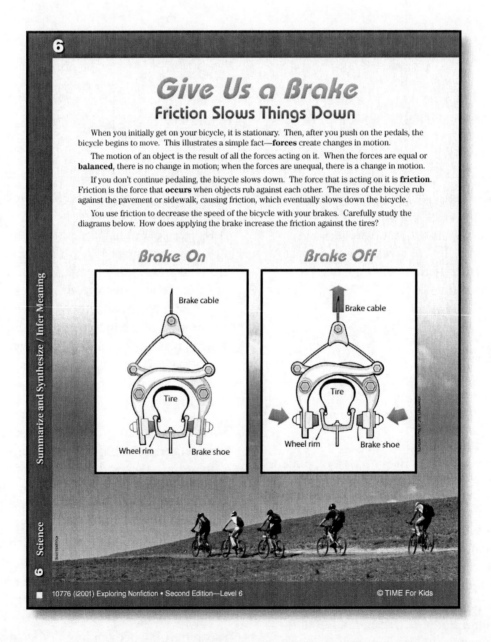

6

Give Us a Brake
Friction Slows Things Down

When you initially get on your bicycle, it is stationary. Then, after you push on the pedals, the bicycle begins to move. This illustrates a simple fact—**forces** create changes in motion.

The motion of an object is the result of all the forces acting on it. When the forces are equal or **balanced**, there is no change in motion; when the forces are unequal, there is a change in motion.

If you don't continue pedaling, the bicycle slows down. The force that is acting on it is **friction**. Friction is the force that **occurs** when objects rub against each other. The tires of the bicycle rub against the pavement or sidewalk, causing friction, which eventually slows down the bicycle.

You use friction to decrease the speed of the bicycle with your brakes. Carefully study the diagrams below. How does applying the brake increase the friction against the tires?

Brake On   **Brake Off**

Brake cable

Brake cable

Tire

Tire

Wheel rim   Brake shoe

Wheel rim   Brake shoe

Summarize and Synthesize / Infer Meaning

Science

6

10776 (i2001) Exploring Nonfiction • Second Edition—Level 6   © TIME For Kids

Analyzing Content-Area Text (cont.)

Planning for Explicit Teaching			
Vocabulary			Language
Specialized Content: • friction	**General Academic:** • result • occur • decrease	**Everyday:** • stationary (stationery) • acting • forces	**Features:** • diagram in text **Functions:** • inference

Specialized Content Vocabulary: *Friction* is probably the only specialized content vocabulary word students might need for this text. Of course, if this word has already been covered earlier in the unit or in a previous unit, the time devoted to it may be minimal.

General Academic Vocabulary: *Result, occur,* and *decrease* are general academic vocabulary words students will need to understand in order to comprehend this small piece of text. They are words that students are likely to encounter time and time again in texts, and students should work to make this part of their oral and written vocabularies.

Everyday Vocabulary: In reading the text, there are three words that are potential stumbling blocks to student understanding: *stationary* (students may know its homophone *stationery*), *acting,* and *forces.* These are examples of words whose meanings are very different in the context of science, as opposed to their use in everyday language. Chances are students could create a quick definition of all three: *stationary* (as something written on), *acting* (in reference to a performance of some sort), and *force* (as pressure or strength applied to something). But in this

context of science, these become frequently used words with very different meanings. In particular, *force* has a similar definition in both everyday language and as used in this text. However, students are more likely to use *force* as a verb, rather than as a noun, as it is used here.

Features of Language: There is not much text on this page, but making meaning from the diagrams on the bottom of the page will be critical to student understanding.

Functions of Language: Students are expected to infer meaning from the diagrams to understand how friction works. Students need to be familiar with *inference* and use the language of inference to explain their understanding.

Resources

• • • • • • • • • • •

Lesson Design Template

Planning for Explicit Teaching

Vocabulary

Specialized Content:

General Academic:

Everyday:

Language

Features:

Functions:

Strategies

Schema and Vocabulary Building:

Comprehensible Input:

Opportunities for Practice:

Schema and Vocabulary Building

Planning for Explicit Teaching			
Vocabulary			Language
Specialized Content:	General Academic:	Everyday:	Features: Functions:
Strategies			
Schema and Vocabulary Building:	Comprehensible Input:		Opportunities for Practice:

How Students Benefit

What Is Schema Building?

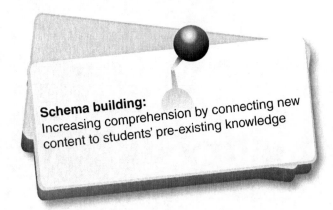

Schema building:
Increasing comprehension by connecting new content to students' pre-existing knowledge

Have you ever been in a class where the information the teacher was presenting seemed completely foreign to you? Think back to a class in high school that was not connected to any class you had taken in prior years—chemistry, for example. How much harder did you have to work to understand and retain the information? This difficulty may have been due to your lack of prior knowledge on the topic. Your teacher could have alleviated your difficulty in attaining the new information if he or she had spent time building your schema on the new topic.

In general, schema building is a technique teachers can use to increase the understanding and retention of content by connecting the new content to *pre-existing* or *prior knowledge*.

Why Is Schema a Critical Component for Comprehension?

Schema is defined by McNeil (1992) as "concepts, beliefs, expectations, processes— virtually everything from past experiences that are used in making sense of reading" (20).

Schema building is an essential tool for teachers because it aids English language learners in their acquisition of academic language. For new information to make sense and be remembered, teachers must first access students' prior knowledge of the content and help them to make relevant connections that will aid in comprehension and retention of the new material. This new information can be textual, content specific, or culturally related.

Research has also shown that information is connected in the brain through mental links that are mapped onto an individual's existing schema. If English language learners are able to create multiple links that are personally meaningful, then information is easier to retain. For this reason, many researchers maintain that it is essential to build on readers' existing schema when introducing them to new content or concepts and that this is especially true for English language learners (Anderson 1984; Droop and Verhoeven 1998; Echevarria, Short, and Powers 2006; Koda 2007).

Schema Building and Culture

Something else to consider when instructing students from cultures other than your own is that a student's schema may be influenced by his or her culture. According to Carrell and Eisterhold, "reading comprehension involves one's knowledge of the world, which may be culturally based and culturally biased" (553). Recent studies have found that when students are tested on passages whose content is culturally familiar, they have much higher scores for comprehension and recall than when the content is culturally unfamiliar (Malik 1990).

How Students Benefit (cont.)

Schema as a Bridge Between Prior and New Knowledge

As primary-language students come to school with a variety of past experiences, so do English language learners. To effectively build students' schema, it is important to provide them with experiences that will act as a bridge between the prior knowledge and the new knowledge.

Students may experience content either **directly** or **vicariously**.

- *Direct experiences* are those in which students have experienced the content concepts and topics firsthand. Some examples of direct experiences would be going to a museum or to the zoo.

- *Vicarious experiences* are those in which a student experiences the content secondhand. Some examples of vicarious experiences would be reading a book on a topic, seeing pictures, viewing realia, and watching a video.

Preassessing Prior Knowledge

Preassessing students allows teachers the opportunity to discover what their students already know about the unit of study. It is important for teachers to recognize preassessing prior knowledge so students can engage in the unit of study as well as prepared as they construct knowledge appropriate to their level.

For instance, if a teacher is planning a unit on friction, he or she will need to consider whether his or her students have already had direct experiences with this material, and design a plan for preassessing his or her students. Some examples of preassessing might include self-assessing students on the unit of study or orally asking students to share what they know about the specific curriculum topic.

Building Schema

While building a student's schema through vicarious experiences and relevant connections to culture, it is important to make connections to vocabulary that represent the important concepts within the topic. The National Literacy Panel recently reviewed research from the field of second-language acquisition and found that focusing on academic vocabulary may enhance second language learners' reading comprehension (Lesaux and Geva 2006).

However, simply exposing English language learners to words is not sufficient for academic literacy; words need to be explicitly taught, and students need time to practice using vocabulary. If we consider what it means to know a word, vocabulary instruction should move beyond a focus on learning definitions of words and toward an emphasis on functional knowledge of words—specifically, how to use them. We must teach meanings through explanation, provide multiple examples of how to use the words correctly, and give ample opportunities for students to practice.

It is also important to consider that explicit instruction on vocabulary can begin from the moment an English language learner sets foot in the classroom. In other words, students do not need to be fluent in English before they can begin to learn academic vocabulary and engage with academic text. On the contrary, providing students with authentic experiences and practice by teaching vocabulary within the content areas can provide a much richer and more meaningful approach to learning vocabulary than a focus on learning words in isolation.

How Students Benefit (cont.)

What Does It Mean to Know a Word?

It is clear that teaching vocabulary is a critical component of supporting English language learners in their mastery of academic language. As teachers select the vocabulary words to share with students during instruction, they need to also think about the ways in which they are going to teach them. Strategies for effective vocabulary instruction are a vital piece of the plan.

Introduction to a word's meaning must go beyond dictionary and glossary definitions; in fact, teachers may skip these types of definitions altogether. That is because dictionary and glossary definitions are generally written to be as concise as possible. This is one of the reasons students have difficulty translating definitions into use, such as writing sentences. The following example demonstrates how dictionary definitions may actually mislead students in determining a word's meaning:

Merriam-Webster defines the word *disrupt* as "break up; split." This could easily be interpreted as physical breaking, as in, " We disrupted the candy bar so we could all share it." Rather than introducing words by sharing the dictionary definition or having students look them up, providing a student-friendly explanation makes word meanings more accessible to all students, but especially to English language learners.

If your class is like many others, your students probably get a few words each week that they are responsible for learning; as the teacher, you most likely assess them on those words at the end of the week or unit. Many students will study the weekly list and score fairly well on a simple test of definitions. This type of routine vocabulary instruction happens in thousands of classrooms every week. Now, ask yourself this: If you tested them on those words at the end of the school year, how many students would still do well? So then, what does it mean to *know* a word? (Beck, McKeown, and Kucan 2002)

Wong-Fillmore and Snow (2000) tell us that knowing a word does indeed mean knowing something about its definition or its core meaning. But how many words have a single meaning or use? Not many, which is why simply knowing the definition of a word is not necessarily the hallmark of knowing the word. Knowing a word involves understanding the following:

- its core meaning (e.g., *digestion* means the process by which the body converts food into energy)

- its derivations or similar forms (e.g., *digest*, *ingest*, *digestive*, *indigestion*)

- its spelling and pronunciation

- its part of speech

- how to use its various forms in sentences

- how it relates to other words and concepts (e.g., *food*, *nutrients*, *intestines*)

How Students Benefit *(cont.)*

Planning Vocabulary Strategies

There are many effective strategies and activities for teaching and practicing vocabulary. Scarcella (2003) suggests teachers ask the following questions to determine the effectiveness of a vocabulary activity:

- Does the strategy teach students the words, strategies, and/or skills they need to know?

- Is there evidence that this strategy works? Do I have evidence or "proof" of student learning as a result of the strategy or activity?

- Is the strategy/activity time efficient? Is the time spent during instruction, practice, and planning justified by the results?

- Is there any research evidence to support using the strategy/activity? Have the strategies/activities been widely or successfully used by others? Are there other teachers who report successful use of this strategy or activity?

- Does the strategy/activity focus on vocabulary depth and/or complexity?

- Does the activity help students learn a strategy they can apply to learning other words?

- Does the activity help students remember the words?

- Does the activity help students to practice the words?

- Do the students enjoy or like the activities? If not, does the benefit of participation in the activity outweigh the risk of turning students off to vocabulary learning?

While the answer to these questions does not have to be a resounding "yes," it is important to consider how you might answer many of them when evaluating the effectiveness of your current or future vocabulary instruction.

To allow students to have a deeper understanding of words, it is important to teach students about words. What this means is that an important part of vocabulary instruction is the teaching of strategies for determining the meaning of a word. Strategies that were found to be successful included relating the word to a cognate, analyzing words for their morphological meaning, and using context clues.

How Students Benefit (cont.)

Cognates

Teaching cognates is a type of schema building that can provide a bridge between words students already know and new words they need to learn. Cognates are words that have common origins. For a list of cognates see pages 88–89.

For example, in a science lesson on reptiles, a teacher might introduce the cognates *venomous* (English) and *venenoso* (Spanish) to English language learners whose primary language is Spanish. (Both words derive from the Sanskrit word *visa*, meaning "poison.") In teaching this pair of cognates, a teacher would likely help students make connections between a word and a concept they have familiarity with in their native language.

While cognates can be a powerful schema-building strategy, just because words look and sound the same does not mean they derive from the same roots. It is important to instruct students about *false cognates*, or words from different languages that sound the same but do not have the same meaning. These words are more commonly known as "false friends" and can be quite confusing for English language learners (e.g., the English *assist*, meaning "to help," and *asistir* in Spanish, which means "to attend"). These words look and sound similar but do not share a common meaning. A humorous example of this is the government official who was speaking to a predominantly Spanish-speaking crowd. He came late to the event and told the crowd that he was *muy embarazada*, which prompted a large laugh from the crowd. Instead of telling the crowd he was very *embarrassed*, he told them that he was very *pregnant*!

Morphology

Morphology, or the study of the content and structure of words, is another strategy that has been found to be helpful for learning new words, which in turn, builds schema. Students can be taught to take words apart to look for the *morphemes* (smallest units of meaning in a word). For instance, in the word *independently*, there are four morphemes: *in-*, *depend*, *-ent*, *-ly*, with *depend* as the root word. The other parts *in-*, *-ent*, and *–ly* are known as *affixes* (prefixes and suffixes). The word *prefix* itself is a model of a word whose meaning can be determined by using morphology. As a prefix, *pre-* means "before," while *fix* as a base word means "to attach or to fasten." Literally, *prefix* means "to attach before something."

There are also several common Greek and Latin roots students can identify to help determine word meaning. For example, *port*, meaning "to carry," influences the meaning of words such as *export*, *transport*, and *portable*. If any of these words are unknown to students, their knowledge of both affixes and roots may help them analyze the word for meaning. To make the most of these strategies, students require scaffolded practice in which teachers have isolated the strategies and provided textual samples that serve as examples for practice.

(See pages 90–96 for root words and affixes.)

How Students Benefit (cont.)

Context Clues

Another strategy that has been found to be helpful in aiding English language learners in acquiring new words and thus building their schema is context clues. Three types of context clues that have been found to be helpful for word identification are picture clues, semantic cues (clues), and syntactic cues (clues) (Roe, Smith, and Burns 2008). Research has shown that the structure and meaning of the sentence can aid in identifying an unknown word; therefore, it is important that word-recognition skills be taught in context.

Picture Clues: Beginning readers and English language learners in the early stage of acquiring the language should use pictures to help them determine the overall meaning of text. One strategy that teachers can use is a Picture Walk. The teacher begins by sharing pictures from the text and making predictions about what may be found in the text. This is a strategy best used for beginning English language learners; learners at later stages should not become reliant upon it. In the context of content-area texts, it's important for students to pay attention to charts, graphs, diagrams, and the captions that accompany pictures.

Semantic Cues: These cues are derived from the words, phrases, and sentences that surround an unknown word. One way teachers can aid students in becoming proficient at using this technique is through a cloze activity (Roe, Smith, and Burns 2008). This requires teachers to remove words from a passage systematically and replace them with blank lines. Students then use the surrounding sentence parts to determine the words that could be placed on the blanks. For instance, *Joey and Sam were playing catch with a _____ and glove. Joey threw the ball so _____ it went over Sam's head.*

Syntactic Cues: These cues are provided by the grammar or structure of language, which can aid students in word recognition. The cloze activity listed above can be modified and used to teach students to pay attention to syntactic clues. To do this, a teacher reads the sentence aloud and still omits the words on the blanks. When using this activity for syntactic clues, teachers should directly instruct students as to the importance of where the word is in the sentence and what part of speech would be represented by the omitted word. For instance, when using the example above, *Joey and Sam were playing catch with a _____ and glove. Joey threw the ball so _____ it went over Sam's head,* the teacher directs students to the part of the sentence where the blank is and asks, "What part of speech would make sense in the blank?"

How Students Benefit (cont.)

Other types of context clues include the following:

Definition Clues: Define the word in a sentence. (e.g., *Monsoons* are big, violent rainstorms that occur seasonally.)

Appositive Clues: Define a word with an explanation, synonym, or actual definition in the sentence. Appositives are generally set off by commas, dashes, or parentheses following the word. (e.g., The Earth *rotates*, or spins, on its axis.)

Comparison Clues: Compare unknown words to words in the sentence that offer clues to the meaning of the unknown words (e.g., A *monsoon* is as likely as other violent storms to bring death and destruction.)

Contrast Clues: A contrast between the unknown words and known words in the sentence can also provide clues to meaning. (e.g., *Jet streams* always flow parallel to the equator but move north or south depending on the time of year.).

Example Clues: Provide examples for words that may be unfamiliar. (e.g., Many storms are predictable and occur *seasonally*, for example, in spring and fall.)

(List adapted from, Roe, Smith, and Burns 2008)

Academic Word Lists

As with many hot topics in education, teachers are being asked to address the issue of academic language instruction with little professional development. As a result, the way we most frequently have seen academic language being addressed is through Academic Word Lists.

There are several lists of academic words, both specialized content and general academic, that students are likely to encounter frequently in academic text. Some of these lists are more general, while others categorize words based on content areas.

Included in the resource section (pages 97–101) as a reference for teachers in planning their instruction is the Academic Word List (AWL). Originally created by Coxhead (2000), the list consists of 570 of the most common words found in academic texts across a range of content areas, excluding the 2,000 words considered part of a basic conversational vocabulary. These words are part of word families and are helpful for students in not only learning the words but having some level of knowledge to access many varities of the specific word. For example, the word *analyze* (see page 97) is on the list because of the multiple variations of how it can appear in academic texts (e.g., *analysis, analytical, analyst*). The list we have included was reordered to group the words by frequency, with Group 1 consisting of the words students will encounter most frequently (Stubbs 2008).

However, distributing any of these lists without instruction is essentially useless to most students. In order to maximize the benefit of these word lists, students must receive explicit instruction on word meanings and usage. Students must be given time for meaningful practice of these words in an academic setting, as imperfect practice on their own will not lead to mastery. At their most effective, these lists can serve as a guide for teachers when trying to select general academic vocabulary for instruction from the classroom text. For students, it can be useful as a reference for further study or in preparing for exams such as the SAT or ACT.

How Students Benefit (cont.)

Enhancing Comprehension Using Schema and Vocabulary

To see how all of these areas can help students when they encounter unfamiliar topics or words, we can take a look at a passage from Lewis Carroll's *Through the Looking-Glass and What Alice Found There* (1902).

> The Jabberwocky sings:
>
> Twas brillig and the slithy toves
> Did gyre and gimble in the wabe;
> All mimsy were the borogoves
> And the mome raths outgrabe.

Here you can see how knowledge of semantics, syntax, sentence structure, and morphology can help us (to some extent) to comprehend the text. As a reader, you can answer simple questions using semantic and syntactic clues. At what time of day did this take place? Brillig. Who was there? The slithy toves. What did they do? Gyre and gimble. Knowledge of syntax helps determine the time of day (*brillig*, noun), who was there (*slithy toves*, noun), and what they did (*gyre* and *gimlet*, verbs).

In addition, while the answers to these questions are nonsense words, the nonsense words actually contain word parts (morphemes) that come from the English language, making them somewhat comprehensible. For instance, the word *slithy* is thought to come from a combination of *slimy* and *slither* (Hofstadter 1980).

Focusing on vocabulary allows students to put labels to their newly attained knowledge. By arming English language learners with these tools for accessing their schema, we are preparing them to learn independently from text.

The following pages describe strategies teachers can use to enhance schema and help build students' academic vocabulary.

Strategies for the Classroom

Quick-Draw

Overview

This strategy provides a way for students to quickly access their schema by drawing a picture. This strategy helps students activate prior knowledge on a particular subject.

Standards

- **McREL:** Students will use level-appropriate vocabulary in speech.

- **TESOL:** Students will use English to obtain, process, construct, and provide subject matter information in spoken and written form.

Directions

To incorporate this strategy, do the following:

1. Prompt students to draw a picture that shows everything they know about a subject.

2. At your signal, students turn to a partner, share their drawings, and discuss the topic. Encourage students to look for similarities and differences between their drawings. Students can share how they know what they know.

3. Students can also add one- or two-word labels to their drawings that capture the big ideas from their background knowledge. (If working with younger students, add the labels.)

4. Collect the drawings and use the information as a preassessment to develop the unit of study. These initial drawings can also be used as a basis of comparison after the unit of study is completed to show growth in knowledge.

Differentiating by Proficiency Level

Beginning:
Provide picture cards to students to activate prior knowledge before they draw.

Intermediate:
Offer sentence frames (see page 120) to be used when students share with their partner.

Advanced:
Ask students to summarize what their partner said. This could also be supported with a sentence frame (see page 120).

Strategies for the Classroom (cont.)

Quick-Draw (cont.)

Below are examples of how this strategy can be incorporated in a lesson.

Grades 1–2

Text Topic: My Community

Example: Students are asked to draw a picture depicting important features that make up a community. For example, a student meets with a partner and shares that in a community there are schools and parks depicted in the sketch. At the end of the unit, students revisit their pictures and use their drawings as a basis of comparison with what they learned.

Grades 3–5

Text Topic: Ecosystems

Example: Students are asked to draw a picture depicting important features of an ecosystem. For example, a student meets with a partner and shares that in an ecosystem there are many organisms as depicted in the sketch. At the end of the unit, students revisit their pictures and use their drawings as a basis of comparison with what they learned.

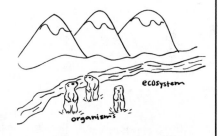

Grades 6–8

Text Topic: American Revolution

Example: Students are asked to draw a picture depicting important features of the American Revolution. At the end of the unit, students revisit their pictures and use their drawings as a basis of comparison with what they learned. For example, a student revisits the quick-draw sketch they made in the beginning of the unit and decides to add the title commander-in-chief to George Washington based on what was learned during the unit.

Strategies for the Classroom (cont.)

Quick-Write

Overview

This strategy provides students with the opportunity to write everything they know about a specific topic. This strategy can work as an informal preassessment in allowing the teacher to have a better understanding of what background knowledge the students possess.

Standards

- **McREL:** Students will use level-appropriate vocabulary in speech.

- **TESOL:** Students will use English to obtain, process, construct, and provide subject matter information in spoken and written form.

Directions

To incorporate this strategy, do the following:

1. Provide a prompt on the upcoming content and give students five minutes to write about the topic.

2. At your signal, ask students to turn to a partner and share their Quick-Writes. Students can look for similarities and differences in their writing and discuss what they know about the topic.

3. Collect the Quick-Writes and use the information as a preassessment to develop the unit of study. These initial Quick-Writes can also be used as a basis of comparison after the unit of study is completed to show growth in knowledge.

Differentiating by Proficiency Level

Beginning:	**Intermediate:**	**Advanced:**
Have students work together for this activity. You may want to do a group-write to construct sentences based on students' responses. Students then turn to their partners and take turns reading what the group wrote.	Provide students with a word bank for the topic that they will study. Students can select words from their bank to complete their Quick-Write.	Have students construct sentences that address the prompt and show what they know about a topic. Encourage students to share their sentences with classmates.

Strategies for the Classroom (cont.)

Quick-Write (cont.)

Below are examples of how this strategy can be incorporated in a lesson.

Grades 1–2

Text Topic: Weather

Example: Students are given the following prompt: *Explain what you know about weather.* Students are also provided with a word bank (e.g., *rain, snow, seasons, sun, weather, temperature*) that they can use to complete their sentences. After completing their sentences, students are then asked to share their Quick-Writes with a partner. For example, a student composes the following Quick-Write: *There are four seasons. In each season the weather changes. Right now it is winter and it is snowing.*

Grades 3–5

Text Topic: Multiplication

Example: Students are given time to write what they know about groups, sets, and products (notice the multiple-meaning word *product*, which the teacher plans to teach explicitly later). Students are once again given a word bank with specific words (e.g., *pattern, sum, digit, factor, multiples*) to help guide them with writing their sentences. After a few minutes, students are given time to share what they have written with a partner. For example, a student composes the following Quick-Write: *Multiplication is repeated addition. There are digits that you have to multiply in order to find the sum.*

Grades 6–8

Text Topic: Human Heart

Example: Before beginning a unit on the human heart, students are given the opportunity to write what they know about the unit. Students are given a word bank (e.g., *muscle, blood, blood vessels, pulse, cells*) to help guide them with writing their sentences. After a few minutes, students are given time to share with a partner what they have written. For example, a student composes the following Quick-Write: *The human heart pumps blood throughout the body. There are several vessels that help transport the blood. You can also feel your pulse on your wrist or on the side of your neck.*

Strategies for the Classroom (cont.)

Quick-Draw/Quick-Write

Overview

This strategy encourages students to use both drawing and writing to represent their knowledge on a topic. The combination of these two strategies allows students to access their schema by using the visual modality and responding to those visuals with the usage of academic language.

Standards

- **McREL:** Students will use level-appropriate vocabulary in speech.

- **TESOL:** Students will use English to obtain, process, construct, and provide subject matter information in spoken and written form.

Directions

To incorporate this strategy, do the following:

1. Provide students with a prompt. Instruct students to draw a picture that represents their knowledge on the topic. After a short period of time, provide a writing prompt that challenges students to be more specific about their knowledge.

2. At your signal, tell students to turn to a partner and share their Quick-Draw/Quick-Writes. Students can look for similarities and differences in their work.

3. Collect the drawings and writings, using the information as a preassessment to develop the unit of study. These initial works can also be used as a basis of comparison after the unit of study is completed to show growth in knowledge.

Differentiating by Proficiency Level

Beginning:	Intermediate:	Advanced:
Share a book on the topic of study before asking students to participate, so that they can be familiar with the unit of study.	Provide students with a word bank to help in constructing their Quick-Write and encourage students to use the vocabulary in their word bank when sharing with classmates.	Have students write a summary about their knowledge on the topic. Remind them that when they write a summary, they should address the questions *What? When? Where? Why?* and *How?*

Strategies for the Classroom (cont.)

Quick-Draw/Quick-Write (cont.)

Below are examples of how this strategy can be incorporated in a lesson.

Grades 1–2

Text Topic: Plants

Example: Before reading a nonfiction book about plants, students are asked to draw a picture to show what they know about plants. Additionally, students are provided with a word bank (e.g., *plant, leaf, roots, petal, grow*) to use when writing. For example, a student's Quick-Write reads *Every plant has roots. As it grows, so do the roots. Sometimes a leaf may sprout.*

Grades 3–5

Text Topic: European Explorers

Example: Before beginning a chapter on European explorers, students are asked to draw a picture that represents what they know about the topic. After a few minutes, students do a Quick-Write about their pictures. Additionally, students are provided with a word bank (e.g., *Europe, overseas, exploration, trade, expedition*) to use when writing. After a few minutes, students are asked to share their writing with a partner. For example, a student writes the following: *Many European explorers went on expeditions. Because they wanted to come to America, they traveled overseas.*

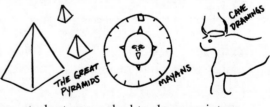

Grades 6–8

Text Topic: Early Civilization

Example: Before beginning a unit on early civilization, students are asked to draw a picture that represents what they know about the topic. After a few minutes, students do a Quick-Write about their pictures. Additionally, students are provided with a word bank (e.g., *Egypt, India, Mesopotamia, trade, economy*) to use when writing. After a few minutes, students are asked to share their writing with a partner. For example, a student writes the following: *Trade was very important during the Early Civilization period. Many countries such as Egypt and India had different goods to offer to other countries.*

Strategies for the Classroom (cont.)

Circle Map

Overview

This strategy allows students to express what they know about a topic either individually or in a group. This strategy helps students activate prior knowledge and make connections between terms related to the new area of topic.

Standards

- **McREL:** Students will use level-appropriate vocabulary in speech.

- **TESOL:** Students will use English to obtain, process, construct, and provide subject matter information in spoken and written form.

Directions

To incorporate this strategy, do the following:

1. Draw a Circle Map. (A Circle Map looks like a doughnut, with the central topic in the center and relevant ideas written around the circle.) This activity is done as a whole class, in small groups, or individually.

2. Write the topic in the center circle. Provide an example or two of ideas relevant to the topic. Write these ideas around the circle. If this activity is done as a whole class or in a small group, ask students to share concepts about the topic. If it is done individually, ask students to add their own ideas to their Circle Map (see page 102).

3. The Circle Map is useful as a preassessment of students' prior knowledge before beginning a unit of study. This activity can also be re-created after the unit of study so that students can add their new knowledge to the map.

Differentiating by Proficiency Level

Beginning:	**Intermediate:**	**Advanced:**
Read a story about the topic of study or provide pictures related to the topic. Once students have been oriented to the appropriate area of study, provide talk time, during which students can share with a partner what they know on the topic.	Have students work in small groups to complete the Circle Map and then come together as a class to contribute to a whole-class map.	Have students work together in small groups to discuss the words they selected for their Circle Maps. Encourage students to defend and support their word choices.

Strategies for the Classroom (cont.)

Circle Map (cont.)

Below is an example of how this strategy can be incorporated in a lesson.

Grades 1-2

Text Topic: Telling Time

Example: Before beginning a unit on telling time, the teacher works with students to create a Circle Map. The Circle Map begins with the word *time* in the center. The word *hour* is added to get the class started. The teacher elicits possible words from the class to add to the Circle Map. When words are suggested, the class discusses whether they agree with the word that is suggested. Students justify their answers with complete sentences.

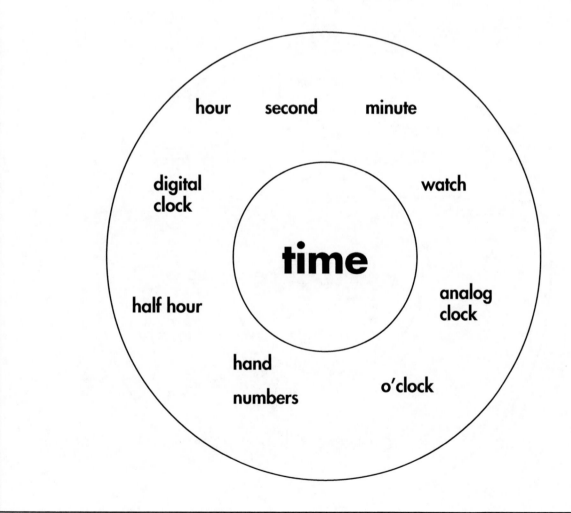

Strategies for the Classroom (cont.)

Circle Map (cont.)

Below is an example of how this strategy can be incorporated in a lesson.

Grades 3-5

Text Topic: Regions

Example: Before beginning a unit on regions, the teacher works with students to create a Circle Map. The Circle Map begins with the word *regions* in the center. The word *west* gets added to get the class started. The teacher elicits possible words from the class to add to the Circle Map. When words are suggested, the class discusses whether they agree with the word that is suggested. Students justify their answers with complete sentences.

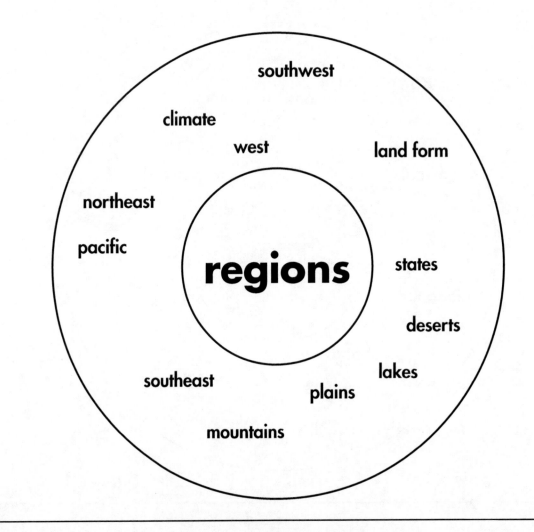

Strategies for the Classroom (cont.)

Circle Map (cont.)

Below is an example of how this strategy can be incorporated in a lesson.

Grades 6-8

Text Topic: Literary Genre

Examples: Before beginning a unit on literary genre, the teacher works with students to create a Circle Map. The Circle Map begins with the word *drama* in the center. The word *audience* gets added to get the class started. The teacher elicits possible words from the class to add to the Circle Map. When words are suggested, the class discusses whether they agree with the word that is suggested. Students justify their answers with complete sentences.

Strategies for the Classroom (cont.)

Semantic Map

Overview

This strategy challenges students to organize words into categories and subcategories that show the relationships among concepts. Using this strategy helps students determine key attributes of a topic and allows them to see how ideas can be categorized.

Standards

- **McREL:** Students will use strategies to organize written work.

- **TESOL:** Students will use English to obtain, process, construct, and provide subject matter information in spoken and written form.

Directions

To incorporate this strategy do the following:

1. Asks students to share what they know about the selected topic of study.

2. As students share, categorize the words. This is best done with the think-aloud method to show the rationale for the categorization. If students do not know all of the terms for the selected categories, it is helpful to explain this information.

3. During the unit of study, the class should revisit their Semantic Maps to add their new knowledge.

Differentiating by Proficiency Level

Beginning:
When preparing the lesson, anticipate which words will most likely appear on the whole-class Semantic Map. Then find pictures that represent these words to present to students.

Intermediate:
Encourage students to tell more about their answers, specifically how their answers relate to the word that is the topic of the Semantic Map.

Advanced:
Have students categorize their own Semantic Maps and explain why and how they selected to categorize their words.

54

Strategies for the Classroom (cont.)

Semantic Map (cont.)

Below is an example of how this strategy can be incorporated in a lesson.

Grades 1–2

Text Topic: Money

Example: Before beginning a unit on money, the teacher works with students to construct a Semantic Map. The Semantic Map begins with the topic word *money* in the center, then the key word *dollar* is added to one of the map lines. The class continues discussing other words, phrases, or symbols they know of that can be added under the word *dollar* (e.g., *100¢*, *bill*, *decimal point*). As keywords are suggested, the class discusses whether they agree with the word that is suggested. Students justify their answers with complete sentences.

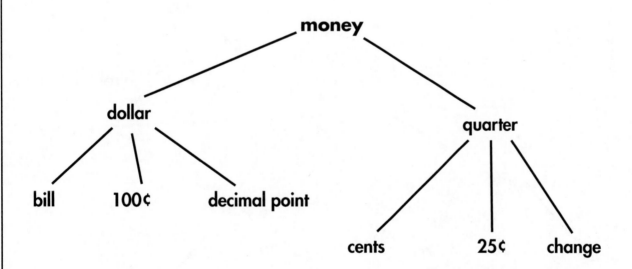

Strategies for the Classroom (cont.)

Semantic Map (cont.)

Below is an example of how this strategy can be incorporated in a lesson.

Grades 3–5

Text Topic: Weather

Example: Before beginning a unit on weather, the teacher works with students to construct a Semantic Map. The Semantic Map begins with the topic word *weather* in the center, then the key word *clouds* is added to one of the map lines. The class continues discussing other words, phrases, or symbols they know of that can be added under the word *weather* (e.g., *cumulus, nimbus*). As keywords are suggested, the class discusses whether they agree with the word that is suggested. Students justify their answers with complete sentences.

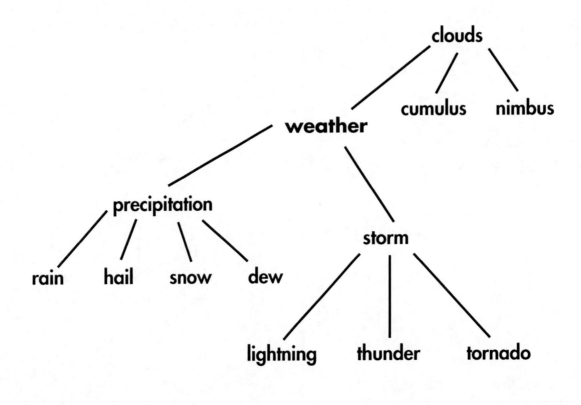

Strategies for the Classroom (cont.)

Semantic Map (cont.)

Below is an example of how this strategy can be incorporated in a lesson.

Grades 6–8

Text Topic: Protozoa

Example: Before beginning a unit on protozoa, the teacher works with students to construct a Semantic Map. The Semantic Map begins with the topic word *protozoa* in the center, then the key word *organism* is added to one of the map lines. The class continues discussing other words, phrases, or symbols they know of that can be added under the word *protozoa* (e.g., *amoeba, paramecium*). As keywords are suggested, the class discusses whether they agree with the word that is suggested. Students justify their answers with complete sentences.

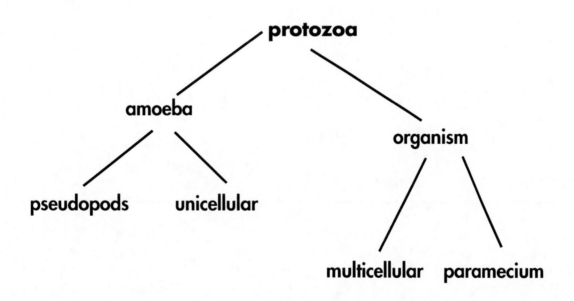

Strategies for the Classroom *(cont.)*

Circle Map/Semantic Map

Overview

With this strategy, students begin to brainstorm using a Circle Map. Once all ideas have been shared, students categorize the words using a Semantic Map. Using this strategy helps students determine key attributes of a topic and allows them to see how ideas can be categorized.

Standards

- **McREL:** Students will use strategies to organize written work.

- **TESOL:** Students will use English to obtain, process, construct, and provide subject matter information in spoken and written form.

Directions

To incorporate this strategy, do the following:

1. Draw a Circle Map (see page 102). This activity is done as a whole class, small group, or individually.

2. Write the topic in the center circle. Provide an example or two of ideas relevant to the topic. Write these ideas around the circle. After completing the Circle Map, discuss how to organize the terms into categories on the Semantic Map with students.

Differentiating by Proficiency Level

Beginning:	Intermediate:	Advanced:
When preparing the lesson, anticipate which words will most likely appear on the whole-class Circle Map/ Semantic Map. Then find pictures that represent these words to present to students.	Have students work together in small groups to discuss the words they selected. Encourage students to discuss in complete sentences.	Have students work in small groups to complete the Circle Map and then come together as a class to contribute to a whole-class map. Guide students in the Semantic Map part of the activity.

58

Strategies for the Classroom (cont.)

Circle Map/Semantic Map (cont.)

Below is an example of how this strategy can be incorporated in a lesson.

Grades 1–2

Text Topic: Measurement

Example: Before beginning a unit on measurement, the teacher works with students to construct a Circle Map. The Circle Map begins with the word *measurement* in the center, then the word *length* is added to get the class started. Students then brainstorm possible words to add to the Circle Map. As words are suggested, the class discusses whether they agree with the word that is suggested. Students justify their answers with complete sentences. Once the Circle Map is completed, the teacher leads the class in creating a Semantic Map using the words from the Circle Map. The word *measurement* is written in the center of the Semantic Map and the words used in the Circle Map are incorporated into the Semantic Map.

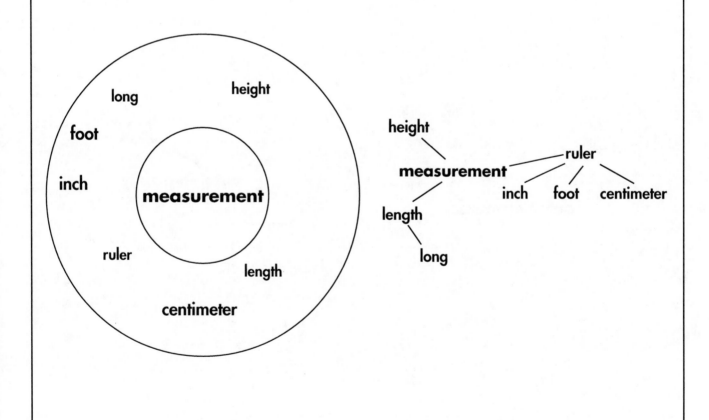

Strategies for the Classroom (cont.)

Circle Map/Semantic Map (cont.)

Below is an example of how this strategy can be incorporated in a lesson.

Grades 3–5

Text Topic: Autobiographical Compositions

Example: Before beginning a unit on writing autobiographical compositions, the teacher works with students to construct a Circle Map. The Circle Map begins with the word *autobiography* in the center, then the word *story* is added to get the class started. Students then brainstorm possible words to add to the Circle Map. As words are suggested, the class discusses whether they agree with the word that is suggested. Students justify their answers with complete sentences. Once the Circle Map is completed, the teacher leads the class in creating a Semantic Map using the words from the Circle Map. The word *autobiography* is written in the center of the Semantic Map and the words used in the Circle Map are incorporated into the Semantic Map.

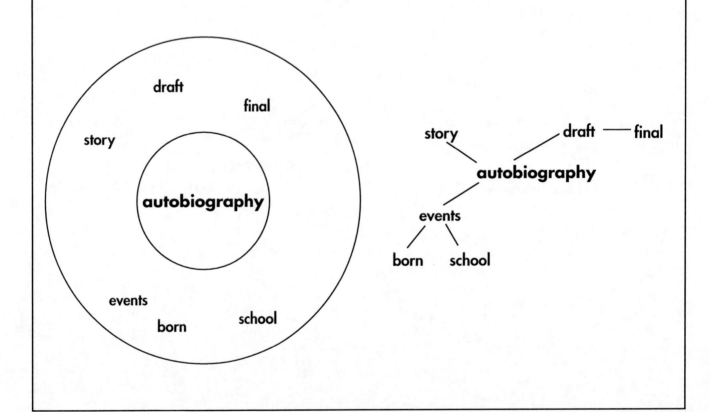

Strategies for the Classroom (cont.)

Circle Map/Semantic Map (cont.)

Below is an example of how this strategy can be incorporated in a lesson.

Grades 6–8

Text Topic: Earth's Composition

Example: Before beginning a unit on the composition of Earth, the teacher works with students to construct a Circle Map. The Circle Map begins with the word *Earth* in the center, then the word *layers* is added to get the class started. Students then brainstorm possible words to add to the Circle Map. As words are suggested, the class discusses whether they agree with the word that is suggested. Students justify their answers with complete sentences. Once the Circle Map is completed, the teacher leads the class in creating a Semantic Map using the words from the Circle Map. The word *Earth* is written in the center of the Semantic Map and the words used in the Circle Map are incorporated into the Semantic Map.

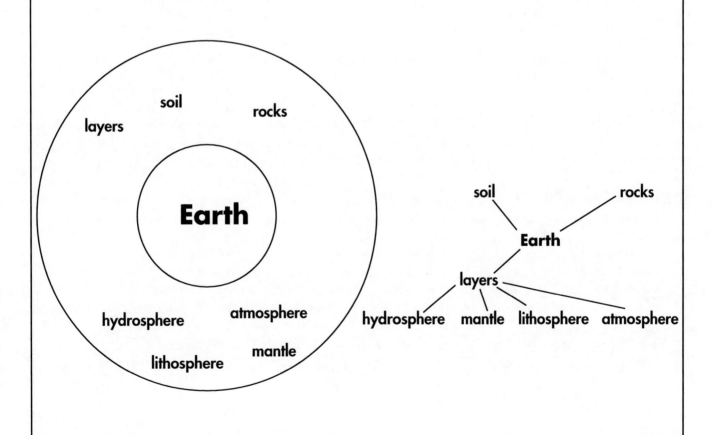

Strategies for the Classroom *(cont.)*

K/W/H/L

Overview

This strategy is a graphic organizer (adapted from Ogle 1986) that allows students to access their prior knowledge and then add to their schema. The *K* stands for "what we know" about a topic. The *W* stands for "what we want to learn" about a topic. The *H* stands for "how we will find the information" about the topic, and the *L* stands for "what we learned" about the topic.

Standards

- **McREL:** Students will use strategies to organize written work.

- **TESOL:** Students will use English to obtain, process, construct, and provide subject matter information in spoken and written form.

Directions

To incorporate this strategy, do the following:

1. Create a chart with four columns. Label the first column *K*, the second column *W*, the third column *H*, and the fourth column *L* (see page 103).

2. Have students brainstorm everything they know about the unit of study and write students' responses in the *K* column.

3. Ask students to share what they want to learn about the unit of study and write students' responses in the *W* column.

4. Finally, before the unit begins, ask students to brainstorm how they will find the information about the topic. Write students' responses in the *H* column.

5. Have students work during the unit to find information to answer their questions about the topic. It is important to remember to revisit the K/W/H/L often throughout the unit to add to the *L* (what we learned) column.

Differentiating by Proficiency Level

Beginning:
Provide students with visuals that depict the topic of study, read aloud a book on the topic, or have them watch a short video on the topic to help build schema.

Intermediate:
Incorporate think-and-talk time. During the think time, provide students with a prompt that allows them to tap the appropriate schema on the topic. After a few minutes, ask students to share what they thought about with a partner.

Advanced:
Ask students to explain how their knowledge about the unit of study has changed. Encourage students to summarize their learning with complete sentences.

Strategies for the Classroom (cont.)

K/W/H/L (cont.)

Below is an example of how this strategy can be incorporated in a lesson.

Grades 1–2

Text Topic: Folktales

Example: Before beginning a unit on folktales, the teacher works with students in creating a K/W/H/L chart. The first three columns are completed prior to learning about folktales. After the lesson is taught, the teacher and students reflect on their learning and complete the last column with what they learned about the lesson topic.

Folktales			
K	**W**	**H**	**L**
What We Know	**What We Want to Know**	**How We Will Find Out**	**What We Have Learned**
• Stories are not true (fiction). • Setting takes place a long time ago. • Stories are creative. • Stories have good and bad characters.	• How many folktales are there? • What do the characters have in common? • How were the stories created? • Who created the stories?	• reading stories • online research • enclopedia	• Tales are from different parts of the world. • Most tales do not have identifiable authors. • Tales started as oral tellings.

Strategies for the Classroom (cont.)

K/W/H/L (cont.)

Below is an example of how this strategy can be incorporated in a lesson.

Grades 3–5

Text Topic: Water Cycle

Example: Before beginning a unit on the water cycle, the teacher works with students in creating a K/W/H/L chart. The first three columns are completed prior to learning about the water cycle. After the lesson is taught, the teacher and students reflect on their learning and complete the last column with what they learned about the lesson topic.

Water Cycle			
K	**W**	**H**	**L**
What We Know	**What We Want to Know**	**How We Will Find Out**	**What We Have Learned**
• Rain comes from clouds. • It snows in the mountains. • Precipitation is another word for rain. • The water cycle is a nonstop cycle.	• What happens to clouds to make it rain? • Why does it snow? • Why don't the oceans overflow?	• science textbooks • online research • trip to the library	• Precipitation happens when a lot of water has condensed and the air cannot hold it anymore. • When water vapor is cooled below freezing point, it snows. • Oceans have large surface areas (no overflow).

Strategies for the Classroom (cont.)

K/W/H/L (cont.)

Below is an example of how this strategy can be incorporated in a lesson.

Grades 6–8

Text Topic: Topography/Erosion

Example: Before beginning a unit on topography/erosion, the teacher works with students in creating a K/W/H/L chart. The first three columns are completed prior to learning about topography/erosion. After the lesson is taught, the teacher and students reflect on their learning and complete the last column with what they learned about the lesson topic.

Topography/Erosion			
K	W	H	L
What We Know	**What We Want to Know**	**How We Will Find Out**	**What We Have Learned**
• Erosion changes shapes of mountains. • Erosion has to do with water. • Erosion happens all the time.	• Why does erosion happen? • What other factors cause erosions?	• science textbooks • online research • trip to the library	• There are five types of erosion: gravity, water, shoreline, ice, and wind. • Erosion happens when running water, sea waves, wind, or glaciers pick up materials from Earth's surface.

Strategies for the Classroom (cont.)

Visual/Vocal

Overview

This strategy involves drawing a simple picture for students at the beginning of a lesson to introduce concepts and vocabulary while discussing the topic and connecting it to background knowledge. The key to this strategy is the thinking aloud, which occurs while the teacher is tracing the picture that was previously drawn.

Standards

- **McREL:** Students will use a variety of strategies to extend reading vocabulary.

- **TESOL:** Students will use English to obtain, process, construct, and provide subject matter information in spoken and written form.

Directions

To incorporate this strategy, do the following:

1. Before beginning a lesson, investigate the concepts and vocabulary words that are necessary for students to be successful within the content.

2. As part of the planning process, pre-sketch a picture that incorporates the relevant information. Make sure to use the vocabulary as labels.

3. As an introduction to the lesson, use a marker to sketch the drawing that was pre-sketched while the students watch (visual). As the elements are drawn do a "think aloud" (vocal) about why these elements are being added to the drawing, making sure to incorporate the relevant vocabulary.

Differentiating by Proficiency Level

Beginning:
Pull students aside before the lesson and conduct the Visual/Vocal activity with them individually. This integrates a slower pace for the drawing, allowing a more meaningful processing time.

Intermediate:
Allow students to re-create the Visual/Vocal activity with partners in a journal to truly demonstrate understanding of the vocabulary and concept.

Advanced:
Allow students to create their own Visual/Vocal drawing. When finished, encourage students to share their Visual/Vocal drawing with the class.

Strategies for the Classroom (cont.)

Visual/Vocal (cont.)

Below is an example of how this strategy can be incorporated in a lesson.

Grades 1–2

Text Topic: Telling Time

Example: While planning a lesson on telling time, the teacher identifies some vocabulary words relevant to the lesson topic (e.g., *clock*, *hour hand*, *minute hand*). In addition, the teacher makes sure that students have a conceptual understanding that 60 minutes equals one hour. With these terms and necessary background knowledge in mind, the teacher creates a simple picture that summarizes the ideas and incorporates the vocabulary while teaching the lesson. The teacher says, "Today we are going to talk about telling time." and proceeds to write *telling time* on the board. The teacher continues by saying, "I can tell time by using a clock. A clock has numbers on it." Then the teacher draws a circle and writes the word *clock* below the circle, as well as the numbers in the correct position. The teacher continues until the sketch has been completely drawn, the main ideas have been summarized, and all of the vocabulary has been incorporated. The teacher proceeds with the lesson, using small clocks as manipulatives that each child can touch to experiment with the concept of telling time.

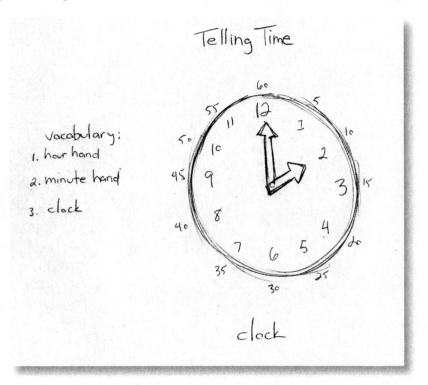

Strategies for the Classroom (cont.)

Visual/Vocal (cont.)

Below is an example of how this strategy can be incorporated in a lesson.

Grades 3–5

Text Topic: Food Chain

Example: While planning a lesson on the food chain, the teacher identifies some vocabulary words relevant to the lesson topic (e.g., *producer, consumer, energy*). In addition, the teacher makes sure that students have a conceptual understanding of the word *chain*. With these terms and necessary background knowledge in mind, the teacher creates a simple picture that summarizes the ideas and incorporates the vocabulary while teaching the lesson. The teacher says, "Today we are going to talk about food chains." and proceeds to write *food chain* on the board. The teacher continues by saying, "A food chain shows how each living thing gets its food. One of the most important parts of a food chain is the sun because the sun provides energy." Then the teacher draws the sun and writes the word *energy* on it. The teacher continues until the sketch has been completely drawn, the main ideas have been summarized, and all of the vocabulary has been incorporated. The teacher proceeds with the lesson by asking students to open their science journals and summarize what was just explained.

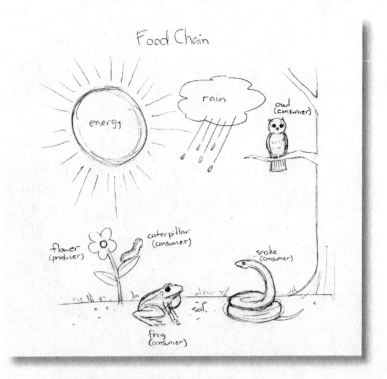

Strategies for the Classroom (cont.)

Visual/Vocal (cont.)

Below is an example of how this strategy can be incorporated in a lesson.

Grades 6-8

Text Topic: World War I

Example: While planning a lesson on World War I, the teacher identifies some vocabulary words relevant to the lesson topic (e.g., *allies*, *alliances*, *The Great War*, *Central Power*). In addition, the teacher makes sure that students have a conceptual understanding of the map of Europe from 1914 to better understand how the location of the different countries was important to the war. With these terms and necessary background knowledge in mind, the teacher creates a simple picture that summarizes the ideas and incorporates the vocabulary while teaching the lesson. The teacher says, "Today we are going to talk about 'The Great War,'" and proceeds to write *The Great War* above the picture. The teacher continues by saying, "In 1914, a war began in Europe. The war began because Archduke Ferdinand, who was going to rule Austria-Hungary, and his wife were visiting Bosnia and were killed by a Serb." Then the teacher draws a map illustrating these places. The teacher continues until the sketch has been completely drawn, the main ideas have been summarized, and all of the vocabulary has been incorporated.

Strategies for the Classroom *(cont.)*

Word Definition Maps

Overview

Word Definition Maps (Scarcella 2003) can help students record different facets of word knowledge in an organized way. Through the development of responses to teacher prompts about a word, students can connect a word to their prior knowledge and expand their knowledge through examples.

Standards

- **McREL:** Students will use a variety of strategies to extend reading vocabulary.

- **TESOL:** Students will use English to obtain, process, construct, and provide subject matter information in spoken and written form.

Directions

To incorporate this strategy, do the following:

1. Think about the unit you are currently teaching or are planning to teach. Brainstorm a list of vocabulary words related to the unit of study. Select one word and label it as the target word.

2. Create a chart with four columns (see page 104). Write the following questions as indicated (insert the target word where the blank appears):

- *What is (a) _____ ?* (first column)

- *What do you know about _____?* (second column)

- *What is an example of _____?* (third column)

- *What is _____ like?* (fourth column)

3. Provide time for students to discuss each question with partners. Then have a class discussion on each question and add responses to the chart together. After each column, create a sentence that answers the question.

Differentiating by Proficiency Level

| **Beginning:** Pull students aside before the lesson and allow them time to access their schema on the target word. Provide pictures or a video that depicts the targeted word. | **Intermediate:** Pair students at this level with strong English-speaking students. The pairing of these students will provide a scaffold. | **Advanced:** Ask students to defend and support their answers as they summarize their learning using complete sentences. |

Strategies for the Classroom (cont.)

Word Definition Maps (cont.)

Below is an example of how this strategy can be incorporated in a lesson.

Grades 1–2

Text Topic: Temperature

Example: During a math lesson, students are learning about temperature. The teacher selects *temperature* as the target word. Students are asked to discuss with a partner the following question: *What is temperature?* After a few minutes, the teacher elicits answers from the class and adds students' responses to the first column. After the answers have been shared, the teacher creates a sentence that explains what temperature is. The teacher continues the process until all four questions and columns are complete.

Temperature			
What is temperature?	**What do you know about temperature?**	**What is an example of temperature?**	**What is temperature like?**
• cold • hot • fever • boiling • not feeling well Temperature is how we measure if something is hot or cold.	• You use a thermometer to measure your temperature. • The temperature is colder in the morning than it is at lunch time. • When the temperature is cold in the mountains, it snows. I know that when I measure temperature, I use a thermometer and it tells us if something is hot or cold.	• Fever is an example of a high temperature. • My mom cooks at a high temperature. • A hot tub has a hot temperature. • Mountains have a cold temperature when it snows. An example of a hot temperature is a hot tub. An example of a cold temperature are the snowy mountains.	**Cold temperature:** • frozen treat • ice cream • ice **Hot temperature:** • soup • my mom's shower A hot temperature is like soup. A cold temperature is like ice cream.

Strategies for the Classroom (cont.)

Word Definition Maps (cont.)

Below is an example of how this strategy can be incorporated in a lesson.

Grades 3-5

Text Topic: American Revolution

Example: During a social studies lesson, students are learning about the American Revolution. The teacher selects *revolt* as the target word. Students are asked to discuss with a partner the following question: *What is a revolt?* After a few minutes, the teacher elicits answers from the class and adds students' responses to the first column. After the answers have been shared, the teacher creates a sentence that explains what a revolt is. The teacher continues the process until all four questions and columns are complete.

Revolt			
What is a revolt?	**What do you know about revolts?**	**What is an example of a revolt?**	**What is a revolt like?**
• riot • battle • disagreement A revolt is when people fight against the people in charge.	• Revolts are hard. • People need a plan to create one. • Revolts usually require a lot of people. I know that revolts are hard and that you need a plan to win.	• Pirates against a captain is an example of a revolt. • Prisoners trying to rebel is an example of a revolt. An example of a revolt is when prisioners try to take over a prison.	• battle • an argument A revolt is like when kids have an argument over who was out in kickball.

Strategies for the Classroom *(cont.)*

Word Definition Maps *(cont.)*

Below is an example of how this strategy can be incorporated in a lesson.

Grades 6–8

Text Topic: Rocks

Example: During a science lesson, students are learning about rocks. The teacher selects *sediment* as the target word. Students are asked to discuss with a partner the following question: *What is sediment?* After a few minutes, the teacher elicits answers from the class and adds students' responses to the first column. After the answers have been shared, the teacher creates a sentence that explains what sediment is. The teacher continues the process until all four questions and columns are complete.

Sediment			
What is sediment?	**What do you know about sediment?**	**What is an example of sediment?**	**What is sediment like?**

• pieces of rock
 	
• pieces of sand
 	
• chunks of mud
 	
• dead plants
 	
Sediment is loose pieces of rock, sand, or other materials.
	• *Sedimentary rocks* has the word *sediment* in it.
	
	• Sediment can be hard or soft.
	
	I know that sedimentary rocks has the word *sediment* in it and sediment can be hard or soft.
		• If you dig a hole at the beach you can find the following:
		
		    • layers of shells
		
		    • fine sand
		
		    • hard wet sand
		
		    • rocks
		
		Sand, a type of sediment, is created as waves or wind smash rocks against each other, breaking them apart.
			• dirt
			
			• soil
			
			• clay
			
			Sediment is like sand, silt, pieces of seashells, minerals, or dead plant matter.

Strategies for the Classroom (cont.)

Everyday to Specialized Content

Overview

This activity helps students differentiate everyday (known) words from academic (specialized content) words. This strategy allows students to see the words used in context correctly. It also helps distinguish the ways proper use of the word is subtly influenced by its meaning in context.

Standards

- **McREL:** Students will use a variety of strategies to extend reading vocabulary.

- **TESOL:** Students will use English to obtain, process, construct, and provide subject matter information in spoken and written form.

Directions

To incorporate this strategy, do the following:

1. Before beginning a lesson, investigate the concepts and vocabulary words that are necessary for students to be successful within the content. Select one of the words and introduce it with a definition that is familiar to students.

2. Provide direct instruction on the new specialized content meaning of the word (how the word will be used in the context of the content-area text).

3. Create an activity sheet where students can practice the everyday and specialized content meanings of the words (see page 105). Make sure the activity sheet includes the following:

- multiple-choice selections that are the focus of the everyday and specialized content vocabulary

- fill-in-the-blank choices, using the word(s) that are the focus of the everyday and specialized content vocabulary

Differentiating by Proficiency Level

Beginning:	**Intermediate:**	**Advanced:**
Use pictures to help represent the everyday and the specialized content defintions and to help demonstrate the difference.	Show students various visuals showing the difference between the multiple meanings.	Ask students to create additional examples of the everyday and specialized content vocabulary words.

74

Strategies for the Classroom (cont.)

Everyday to Specialized Content (cont.)

Below is an example of how this strategy can be incorporated in a lesson.

Grades 1–2

Text Topic: Problem Solving/Probability Statistics

Example: In preparing for a lesson on probability and statistics, the teacher reviews the text and notices that the words *table* and *order* are used in a way with which students might not be familiar. The teacher plans to provide direct instruction on the two words. In addition, an activity sheet is created with multiple examples.

Schema and Vocabulary Building

Resources

Name: _____

Directions: Match the definitions to the vocabulary words below. Decide which meaning is the best specialized content meaning for this math unit.

A.   To go to a restaurant and ask for food

B.   Where I eat dinner

C.   To put things one after another

D.   When the person in charge has everything under control

E.   A way to organize information

F.   To wait to do things later

Word	Everyday Meanings	Specialized Content Meanings
Order	A	C
	D	
Table	B	E
	F	

Directions: Fill in the word that best completes the sentence.

1.   I put the plates on the ____table____ .

2.   Our waiter took our ____order____ .

3.   The numbers were put in the ____table____ to see the results.

4.   I put all of the numbers in ____order____ from least to greatest.

#50631—Building Academic Language   ©Shell Education

Strategies for the Classroom (cont.)

Everyday to Specialized Content (cont.)

Below is an example of how this strategy can be incorporated in a lesson.

Grades 3–5

Text Topic: Geology

Example: In preparing for a lesson on geology, the teacher reviews the text and notices that the words *plate* and *crust* are used in a way with which students might not be familiar. The teacher plans to provide direct instruction on the two words. In addition, an activity sheet is created with multiple examples.

Schema and Vocabulary Building

Resources

Name: _____

Directions: Match the definitions to the vocabulary words below. Decide which meaning is the best specialized content meaning for this math unit.

A. What food is served on

B. What is on top of a pie

C. What I run to in baseball

D. A hard external coating

E. The outer layer of Earth

F. A section of Earth's lithosphere

Word	Everyday Meanings	Specialized Content Meanings
plate	A	F
	C	
crust	B	E
	D	

Directions: Fill in the word that best completes the sentence.

1. I put the ___plate___ on the table.

2. I love a flaky ___crust___ on a pie.

3. The mud had formed a ___crust___ on my shoe.

4. I ran to home ___plate___.

#50631—Building Academic Language   ©*Shell Education*

Strategies for the Classroom *(cont.)*

Everyday to Specialized Content *(cont.)*

Below is an example of how this strategy can be incorporated in a lesson.

Grades 6–8

Text Topic: Exponents

Example: In preparing for a lesson on exponents, the teacher reviews the text and notices that the words *square* and *power* are used in a way with which students might not be familiar. The teacher plans to provide direct instruction on the two words. In addition, an activity sheet is created with multiple examples.

Schema and Vocabulary Building

Resources

Name: _____

Directions: Match the definitions to the vocabulary words below. Decide which meaning is the best specialized content meaning for this math unit.

   A.   The ability to do something

   B.   Strength

   C.   An open place or area

   D.   To bring into agreement

   E.   The product of a number, multiplied by itself

   F.   Number of times as indicated by an exponent that a number occurs as a factor

Word	Everyday Meanings	Specialized Content Meanings
square	C	F
	D	
power	A	E
	B	

Directions: Fill in the word that best completes the sentence.

   1.   If you multiply 2 to the third ___power___ the answer is 8.

   2.   We met near the coffee shop in the town ___square___.

   3.   The ___square___ of 4 is 16.

   4.   The President is given the ___power___ to declare a state of emergency.

#50631—Building Academic Language   ©*Shell Education*

Strategies for the Classroom (cont.)

Illustration of Differing Meanings

Overview

This strategy requires students to draw pictures to represent the different meanings they know for multiple words. This strategy allows students to see the words used in context correctly. It also helps distinguish the ways proper use of the word is subtly influenced by its meaning in context.

Standards

- **McREL:** Students will use a variety of strategies to extend reading vocabulary.

- **TESOL:** Students will use English to obtain, process, construct, and provide subject matter information in spoken and written form.

Directions

To incorporate this strategy, do the following:

1. Review the upcoming unit for words that may have multiple meanings (everyday and specialized content).

2. Provide instruction on the different meanings of the word(s), noting that sometimes its part of the speech may change.

3. Ask students to illustrate the different meanings of the words in a flip book, on cards, or on a graphic organizer. An illustration can be a visual or graphic representation that helps distinguish the words' multiple meanings.

Differentiating by Proficiency Level

Beginning:
Provide multiple examples of the word in its different usages. Share photographs, video, realia, or have students act out a word's meanings.

Intermediate:
Ask students to work in groups to create pictures. Have students add sentences for each word, explaining what the picture represents. Also point out the different parts of speech the word is representing.

Advanced:
Use pictures as support for a discussion on the multiple meanings of a word. After having drawn pictures and written sentences for the word, students can participate in a conversation based on a prompt that is provided to them.

Strategies for the Classroom (cont.)

Illustration of Differing Meanings (cont.)

Below is an example of how this strategy can be incorporated in a lesson.

Grades 1–2

Text Topic: Number Sense—Whole Numbers

Example: The teacher introduces the word *order*. Multiple meanings (everyday and specialized content) are shared with students (e.g., to request food, to give a command, to put things in sequence). Students then create a whole-class illustration for the math (specialized content) meaning of the word. Students then work independently to create pictures for the more common (everyday) meanings.

Strategies for the Classroom (cont.)

Illustration of Differing Meanings (cont.)

Below is an example of how this strategy can be incorporated in a lesson.

Grades 3–5

Text Topic: American Revolution

Example: The teacher introduces the word *soil*. Multiple meanings (everyday and specialized content) are shared with students (e.g., dirt around a tree, to be unclean, a country or region). Students then create a whole-class illustration for the social studies (specialized) meaning of the word. Students then work independently to create pictures for the more common (everyday) meanings.

Strategies for the Classroom *(cont.)*

Illustration of Differing Meanings *(cont.)*

Below is an example of how this strategy can be incorporated in a lesson.

Grades 6–8

Text Topic: Exponents

Example: The teacher introduces the word *square*. Multiple meanings (everyday and specialized content) are shared with students (e.g., a central area in a town, a shape with four sides, the second power of a number). Students then create a whole-class illustration for the math (specialized) meaning of the word. Students then work independently to create pictures for the more common (everyday) meanings.

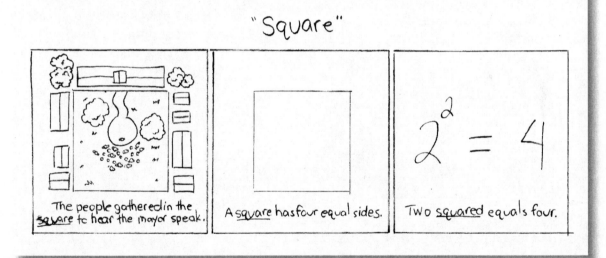

"Square"

The people gathered in the square to hear the mayor speak.

A square has four equal sides.

Two squared equals four.

$$2^2 = 4$$

Strategies for the Classroom (cont.)

Writing or Discussion Prompts

Overview

This strategy requires students to answer a teacher's prompt or question while incorporating academic words from their unit of study. This strategy helps students activate prior knowledge and make connections between terms related to the new area of study.

Standards

- **McREL:** Students will use a variety of strategies to extend reading vocabulary.

- **TESOL:** Students will use English to obtain, process, construct, and provide subject matter information in spoken and written form.

Directions

To incorporate this strategy do the following:

1. Review the upcoming unit for vocabulary that needs to be explicitly taught.

2. After explicitly teaching the vocabulary and spending time teaching the concept of the unit, select a few words to focus on for the prompt.

3. Provide a prompt and the words selected to use in the response sentences.

4. Have students work independently or in small groups to create sentences that answer the prompt, and use the selected words. Once students have created their sentences, they can use them to participate in a discussion.

Differentiating by Proficiency Level

Beginning:
Provide multiple examples to students. For this activity, you may want to pull beginning English language learners in a small group to guide them in the activity using a "think aloud" of all of the sentences.

Intermediate:
Give students the prompt they will be asked to write about and allow students a few minutes to jot down some of their thoughts. Encourage students to use these notes to complete their answers to the prompt.

Advanced:
Ask students to write a summary of what was discussed. When finished, encourage students to share their writing with classmates.

Strategies for the Classroom *(cont.)*

Writing or Discussion Prompts *(cont.)*

Below is an example of how this strategy can be incorporated in a lesson.

Grades 1–2

Text Topic: Probability/Statistics

Example: Students are completing an introductory lesson on probability and statistics. The teacher has students practice their use of the targeted vocabulary by providing them with a prompt to create sentences that incorporate the vocabulary. After the class works together to solve the word problems, students write about their work and then use their writing pieces to have a discussion with classmates.

Targeted Vocabulary:	Sentences:
chart—a graph that shows information **table**—a graph that uses rows and columns **order**—a way to list information **Prompt**: Explain how you used the chart to create a table that put the animals in order.	First, I found the information about the speed of the animals on the chart. Then I drew a table and put the speed of the animals in order.

Strategies for the Classroom (cont.)

Writing or Discussion Prompts (cont.)

Below is an example of how this strategy can be incorporated in a lesson.

Grades 3–5

Text Topic: Erosion

Example: Students are completing an experiment on erosion. The teacher has students practice their use of the targeted vocabulary by providing them with a prompt to create sentences that incorporate the vocabulary. After the class works together on the experiment, students write about their work and then use their writing pieces to have a discussion with classmates.

Targeted Vocabulary:	Sentences:
sample—a small part of what you want to investigate	First, we used a small amount of soil as a sample for the experiment.
soil—a part of Earth's surface, the ground	Next, we put the soil tray on a block so it was tilted.
erosion—the process of Earth's surface being worn away	Then, we poured water on the soil and the water ran down the soil.
	The soil moved down the tray with the water.
Prompt:	Finally, we saw erosion of the soil.
Explain how you completed the experiment that demonstrated erosion.	

Strategies for the Classroom (cont.)

Writing or Discussion Prompts (cont.)

Below is an example of how this strategy can be incorporated in a lesson.

Grades 6–8

Text Topic: Civil War

Example: Students are reading about the Civil War. The teacher has students practice their use of the targeted vocabulary by providing them with a prompt to create sentences that incorporate the vocabulary. After reading the text, students write about the Civil War and then use their writing pieces to have a discussion with classmates.

Targeted Vocabulary:	Sentence:
secede—to break away or leave from a group **launch**—to get something started or set something into action **rebellion**—resistance to or defiance of an authority, such as government	Abraham Lincoln faced the south seceding from the Union over the issue of slavery. Abraham Lincoln appointed and replaced his generals often because he wanted commanders who could win battles, pursue defeated armies, and engage the enemy no matter the cost in lives or materials.
Prompt: Describe some of the problems Abraham Lincoln faced when he became president in March, 1861.	

Strategies for the Classroom (cont.)

Is It Possible?

Overview

Is It Possible? (Blachowitz and Fisher 2002) requires students to determine whether words are being used correctly in a sentence. Students are given several sentences that contain both examples and nonexamples of vocabulary words in context, and must decide if each sentence is possible, or correct. In order for students to determine whether the sentence is possible, they not only need to know the meaning of the word, but must analyze how it is being used as well.

Standards

- **McREL:** Students will use specific strategies to clear up confusing parts of a text.

- **TESOL:** Students will use English to obtain, process, construct, and provide subject matter information in spoken and written form.

Directions

To incorporate this strategy, do the following:

1. Preview the text for vocabulary that needs to be explicitly taught.

2. After explicitly teaching the vocabulary, provide example and nonexample sentences using the vocabulary to practice (e.g., The *staunchly* built house collapsed in a storm; The *treasurer* gave a report at the board meeting; The canary breathed slowly through its *gills*.)

3. Ask students to work independently or in groups to determine which words are used correctly. After a few minutes, conduct a discussion as to why a sentence is possible. When students are familiar with the activity, ask them to create sentences for their classmates to analyze.

Differentiating by Proficiency Level

Beginning:
Provide multiple examples of the selected words to students. Do a "think aloud" of all of the sentences as students follow along.

Intermediate:
For the share portion of this activity, pair intermediate English language learners with strong English-speaking students. The pairing of these students provides a scaffold for the intermediate English language learner.

Advanced:
Ask students to create the sentences for the upcoming activity. While creating these sentences, students can practice using the word in different parts of speech.

Strategies for the Classroom (cont.)

Is It Possible? (cont.)

Below are examples of how this strategy can be incorporated in a lesson.

Grades 1–2

Text Topic: Story Elements

Example: Before reading the selected text to the class, the teacher selects vocabulary to explicitly teach (e.g., *setting*, *narrator*). Students work in groups to determine whether the words are used correctly.

The *narrator* told the story in detail. (possible)

The *setting* of the story was red. (not possible)

Grades 3–5

Text Topic: Food Chains

Example: Before reading the selected text about food chains to the class, the teacher selects vocabulary to explicitly teach (e.g., *omnivore*, *herbivore*). Students work in groups to determine whether the words are used correctly.

The *omnivore* had a leaf for lunch and a mouse for dinner. (possible)

The *herbivore* ate the mouse. (not possible)

Grades 6–8

Text Topic: Global Trade

Example: Before reading the selected text about global trade to the class, the teacher selects vocabulary to explicitly teach (e.g., *foreign*, *route*). Students work in groups to determine whether the words are used correctly.

Some spices were *foreign* because they were created in the same country. (not possible)

Having several *routes* made it easy to move goods from one place to another. (possible)

Resources

● ● ● ● ● ● ● ● ● ●

Cognates List

English	Spanish
angular	angular
author	autor
battle	batalla
conflict	conflicto
empire	imperio
factor	factor
horizontal	horizontal
kilogram	kilogramo
list	lista
map	mapa
margin	margen
object	objeto
quarter	cuarto
second	segundo
telescope	telescopio
temperature	temperatura
thesis	tesis
tunnel	túnel
ultimate	último
united	unido
velocity	velocidad
verb	verbo
victory	victoria

Resources (cont.)

Cognates List (cont.)

English	German
acute	akut
alphabetic	alphabetisch
compass	kompass
compromise	kompromiss
data	daten
decimal	dezimal
electron	elektron
fable	fabel
fabrication	fabrikation
glossary	glossar
helium	helium
hurricane	hurrikan
kilogram	kilogramm
kilometer	kilometer
latin	latein
margin	margen
microscope	mikroskop
million	million
mineral	mineral
muscle	muskel
music	musik
nature	natur
reaction	reaktion
regular	regulär
revolution	revolution

Resources (cont.)

Root Words

Roots and Their Meanings	Examples
a (not)	atypical, abnormal, abridge
act (do)	action, activity, react, interaction
aero (air)	aerobics, aerodynamic, aeronautics
alter (other)	alternative, altercation, alterego
anim (life, spirit)	animal, animate, animosity, inanimate
annu, enni (year)	annual, anniversary, biennial, millenium
aqua (water)	aquarium, aquatic, aquamarine, aquarius
astr (star)	astronaut, astronomy, disaster, asterisk, asteroid
audi (hear)	audience, auditorium, audible, audition, audiovisual
bene (good)	benefit, benefactor, beneficial
bi (two)	bicycle, biennial, binoculars
biblio (book)	bibliography, bible, bibliophile, bibliotherapy
bio (life)	biology, biography, biochemistry, biopsy, biosphere
cardi, cord (heart)	cardiac, cardiology, cardiovascular, cordial, accord, concord, discord
chron (time)	chronological, synchronize, chronicle, chronic
claim, clam (shout)	proclaim, exclaim, acclaim, clamor, exclamation
cogn (know)	recognize, incognito, cognition, cognizant
corp (body)	corporation, corpse, corps, corpuscle, corpus
cosm (world, order)	cosmonaut, cosmos, cosmopolitan, microcosm
cred (believe)	credit, discredit, incredible, credential, credulous
cycl (wheel)	bicycle, cyclone, cycle, encyclopedia, recycle
dem (people)	democracy, demagogue, demography
dic (speak)	dictate, predict, contradict, verdict, diction
doc (teach)	doctrine, document, doctor, indoctrinate, docile

Resources (cont.)

Root Words (cont.)

Roots and Their Meanings	Examples
don, *donat* (give)	donation, donor, pardon, donate
duc (lead)	duct, conduct, educate, induct, aqueduct
eco (house, environment)	ecology, economics, ecosystem
equ (even)	equal, equator, equality
fac, *fic* (make, do)	factory, manufacture, facsimile, efficient, proficient, sufficient
flect, *flex* (bend)	reflect, deflect, reflection, inflection, genuflect, reflex, flexible
form (shape)	form, uniform, transform, reform, formal
gen (give birth)	generation, generate, genocide, progeny, genealogy
geo (earth)	geography, geometry, geology, geophysics
grad (step, go)	gradient, grade, gradual
gram (write, draw)	telegram, diagram, grammar, epigram, monogram
gran (grain)	granule, granola, granary
graph (write)	photograph, phonograph, autograph, biography, graphite
herb (grass)	herbicide, herbivore, herbal
hospit (host)	hospital, hospitality, hospice
hydr/o (liquid, water)	hydroponics, hydraulic
iatr (doctor)	pediatrician, psychiatry, podiatry, geriatrics
infra (beneath, below)	infrastructure, infrared, infrasonic
inter (between, among)	international, intersect, interaction, intercept
judic, *jur*, *jus* (law)	judicious, judge, jury, justice
junct (join)	juncture, conjunction, adjunct, injunction
kilo (thousand)	kilogram, kilobyte, kilometer
kine, *cine* (movement)	kinetics, kinesiology, telekinesis, cinema
labor (work)	labor, laboratory, collaborate, elaborate

Resources (cont.)

● ● ● ● ● ● ● ● ● ● ● ● ● ● ●

Root Words (cont.)

Roots and Their Meanings	Examples
liber (free)	liberty, liberal, liberate
loc (place)	location, locate, dislocation, allocate, local
log (word)	monologue, logic, morphological
lun (moon)	lunar, lunatic, lunacy
lust (shine)	luster, illustrate, lackluster, illustrious
manu (hand)	manual, manufacture, manuscript, manipulate
mar (sea)	marine, submarine, mariner, maritime
memor	memory, memorial
ment (mind)	mental, mention
meter (measure)	metric, thermometer, centimeter, diameter, barometer
migr (wander)	migrate, immigrant, emigrate, migratory
morph (shape)	morphology, amorphous, metamorphoses, anthropomorphic
mot, mov (move, motion)	mobile, automobile, mobilize, motion, motor, promote, demote, motile, remove, movement
mort (death)	mortician, mortal, immortal, mortify
nat (born)	natal, native, nation, nativity, innate
naut (ship)	nautical, astronaut
neg (no)	negative, negate, renege
neo (new)	neophyte, neonatal, neoclassic
ob, os (in the way, against)	object, opposition, obstinate, obstreperous, ostentatious
onym (name)	pseudonym, synonym, antonym, anonymous
or (mouth)	oral, orator
ori (rise, to be born)	origin, original, originate, aborigine
ortho (straight)	orthodontist, orthodox, orthopedist, orthography
pater, patr (father)	paternal, paternity, patricide, patriarch

92

Resources (cont.)

Root Words (cont.)

Roots and Their Meanings	Examples
path (suffering)	pathology, pathogen, sympathy, empathy
ped (foot)	pedal, pedestrian, biped, pedestal
pend (hang)	pendant, pendulum, suspend, append, appendix
phil (love)	philosophy, philanthropist, philharmonic, anglophile
photo (light)	photograph, telephoto, photosynthesis, photogenic
popu (people)	population, populace, popular
port (carry)	portable, transport, import, export, porter
quesit, quer, quisit (search, seek)	question, inquest, request, query, inquisitive
quot (how many, how great)	quote, quota, quotient
radi (beam, space)	radius, radio, radiation, radium, radiator, radiology
rect (straight)	erect, rectangle, rectify, correct
rid (laugh)	ridiculous, deride, ridicule
rod, ros (gnaw)	corrode, erosion
rupt (break)	rupture, erupt, interrupt, abrupt, bankrupt
san (health)	sanitary, sanitation, sane, insanity, sanitarium
scend (climb)	ascend, descend, transcend, descent
sci (know)	science, conscience, conscious, omniscient
scop (see)	microscope, telescope, periscope, stethoscope
scrib, script (write)	inscribe, describe, prescribe, transcript, scripture
sect (cut)	section, dissect, intersect, sect, bisect
sens, sent (think, feel)	sensation, sense, sensitive, sensible, sensory
serv (save, keep, serve)	serve, servant, service, servile
sign (sign)	signal, signature, significant, insignia
simil (like)	similar, simultaneous, simulate, simile
sist (stand)	consist, resist, subsist, assist

Resources (cont.)

Root Words (cont.)

Roots and Their Meanings	Examples
sol (alone)	solo, solitary, desolate, soliloquy
solv (loosen)	dissolve, solve, solvent, resolve
son (sound)	sonar, sonata, sonnet, unison, sonorous
soph (wise)	philosopher, sophomore, sophisticated, sophist
spec (see)	inspect, suspect, respect, spectator, spectacle
struct (build)	structure, construct, instruct, destruction
sum (under, below)	summit, summary, sum, summons
surg, surr (rise)	surge, insurgent, resurgent, resurrect, insurrection, resurrection
tact (touch)	tactile, intact, contact, tact
tele (*far, end*)	telescope, telegram, telephone
terr (land)	territory, terrain, terrestrial, terrace
therm (heat)	thermometer, thermal, thermostat, thermos
tract (pull, drag)	tractor, attract, subtract, traction, extract, contract
trib (pay, bestow)	contribute, tribute, tributary, attribute
urb (city)	urban, suburb, urbane, suburban
vac (empty)	vacancy, vacation, vacuum
verb (word)	verbal, verbatim, verbosity
vert, vers (turn)	convert, inversion, invert, vertical
vid, vis (see)	evidence, provide, providence, visible
viv (live)	revive, survive, livid
volv (roll)	revolve, involve, evolve, revolver
vor (eat)	carnivore, herbivore, omnivore
zo (animal, living being)	protozoa, zoo, zoology

Resources *(cont.)*

Affixes

Prefixes	Meanings	Examples
anti-	against	antiwar
de-	down, off of	destroy
dis-	not, apart	disagree
en(m)-	in, on	encode, embrace
fore-	outside	forecast
in(m)-	in	intake, implant
in-, im-, il-, ir-	not	injustice, impossible, illiterate, irregular
inter-	between	interact
mid-	middle	midway
mis-	wrongly	mistake
non-	not	nonsense
over-	excessive, above	overlook
pre-	before	preview
re-	again	return
semi-	half	semicircle
sub-	under	submarine
super-	above	superstar
trans-	across	transport
un-	not	unfriendly
under-	under	undercover

Resources (cont.)

Affixes (cont.)

Suffixes	Meanings	Examples
-able, -ible	can be done	doable
-al, -ial	quality, relation	personal
-ar, -er, -or	one who	beggar, doer, actor
-ed	past verb	turned
-en	material, make	golden
-er	more	higher
-est	most	best, biggest
-ful	full of	careful, joyful
-ic	quality, relation	linguistic
-ing	present participle	running
-(t)ion	condition, action	action
-(i)ty	state of	infinity, sanity
-(t)ive	having the quality of	motive, votive
-less	without	fearless, careless
-ly	having	quickly, quietly
-ment	mental, mention	enjoyment
-ness	state of	kindness
-ous	full of	joyous, religious
-s	more than one	books
-y	having	happy, windy

Resources

● ● ● ● ● ● ● ● ● ● ● ●

Academic Word Lists

Group 1					
analyze	approach	area	assess	assume	authority
available	benefit	concept	consist	constitute	context
contract	create	data	define	derive	distribute
economy	environment	establish	estimate	evident	export
factor	finance	formula	function	identify	income
indicate	individual	interpret	involve	issue	labor
legal	legislate	major	method	occur	percent
period	policy	principle	proceed	process	require
research	respond	role	section	sector	significant
similar	source	specific	structure	theory	vary

Group 2					
achieve	acquire	administrate	affect	appropriate	aspect
assist	category	chapter	commission	community	complex
compute	conclude	conduct	consequent	construct	consume
credit	culture	design	distinct	element	equate
evaluate	feature	final	focus	impact	injure
institute	invest	item	journal	maintain	normal
obtain	participate	perceive	positive	potential	previous
primary	purchase	range	region	regulate	relevant
reside	resource	restrict	secure	seek	select
site	strategy	survey	text	tradition	transfer

Adapted from Coxhead (2000)

Resources (cont.)

●●●●●●●●●●●●●●●●

Academic Word Lists (cont.)

Group 3					
alternative	circumstance	comment	compensate	component	consent
considerable	constant	constrain	contribute	convene	coordinate
core	corporate	correspond	criteria	deduce	demonstrate
document	dominate	emphasis	ensure	exclude	framework
fund	illustrate	immigrate	imply	initial	instance
interact	justify	layer	link	locate	maximize
minor	negate	outcome	partner	philosophy	physical
proportion	publish	react	register	rely	remove
scheme	sequence	sex	shift	specify	sufficient
task	technical	technique	technology	valid	volume

Group 4					
access	adequate	annual	apparent	approximate	attitude
attribute	civil	code	commit	communicate	concentrate
confer	contrast	cycle	debate	despite	dimension
domestic	emerge	error	ethnic	goal	grant
hence	hypothesis	implement	implicate	impose	integrate
internal	investigate	job	label	mechanism	obvious
occupy	option	output	overall	parallel	parameter
phase	predict	principal	prior	professional	project
promote	regime	resolve	retain	series	statistic
status	stress	subsequent	sum	summary	undertake

Adapted from Coxhead (2000)

Resources (cont.)

Academic Word Lists (cont.)

Group 5					
academy	adjust	alter	amend	aware	capacity
challenge	clause	compound	conflict	consult	contact
decline	discrete	draft	enable	energy	enforce
entity	equivalent	evolve	expand	expose	external
facilitate	fundamental	generate	generation	image	liberal
license	logic	margin	medical	mental	modify
monitor	network	notion	objective	orient	persepective
precise	prime	psychology	pursue	ratio	reject
revenue	stable	style	substitute	sustain	symbol
target	transit	trend	version	welfare	whereas

Group 6					
abstract	accurate	acknowledge	aggregate	allocate	assign
attach	author	bond	brief	capable	cite
cooperate	discriminate	display	diverse	domain	edit
enhance	estate	exceed	expert	explicit	federal
fee	flexible	furthermore	gender	ignorant	incentive
incidence	incorporate	index	inhibit	initiate	input
instruct	intelligence	interval	lecture	migrate	minimum
ministry	motive	neutral	nevertheless	overseas	precede
presume	rational	recover	reveal	scope	subsidy
tape	trace	transform	transport	underlie	utilize

Adapted from Coxhead (2000)

Resources (cont.)

Academic Word Lists (cont.)

Group 7					
adapt	adult	advocate	aid	channel	chemical
classic	comprehensive	comprise	confirm	contrary	convert
couple	decade	definite	deny	differentiate	dispose
dynamic	eliminate	empirical	equip	extract	file
finite	foundation	globe	grade	guarantee	hierarchy
identical	ideology	infer	innovate	insert	intervene
isolate	media	mode	paradigm	phenomenon	priority
prohibit	publication	quote	release	reverse	simulate
sole	somewhat	submit	successor	survive	thesis
topic	transmit	ultimate	unique	visible	voluntary

Group 8					
abandon	accompany	accumulate	ambiguous	append	appreciate
arbitrary	automate	bias	chart	clarify	commodity
compliment	conform	contemporary	contradict	crucial	currency
denote	detect	deviate	displace	drama	eventual
exhibit	exploit	fluctuate	guideline	highlight	implicit
induce	inevitable	infrastructure	inspect	intense	manipulate
minimize	nuclear	offset	paragraph	plus	practitioner
predominant	prospect	radical	random	reinforce	restore
revise	schedule	tense	terminate	theme	thereby
uniform	vehicle	via	virtual	visual	widespread

Adapted from Coxhead (2000)

Resources (cont.)

Academic Word Lists (cont.)

Group 9					
accommodate	analogy	anticipate	assure	attain	behalf
bulk	cease	coherent	coincide	commence	compatible
concurrent	confine	controversy	converse	device	devote
diminish	distort	duration	erode	ethic	format
founded	inherent	insight	integral	intermediate	manual
mature	mediate	medium	military	minimal	mutual
norm	overlap	passive	portion	preliminary	protocol
qualitative	refine	relax	restrain	revolution	rigid
route	scenario	sphere	subordinate	supplement	suspend
team	temporary	trigger	unify	violate	vision

Group 10					
adjacent	albeit	assemble	collapse	colleague	compile
conceive	convince	depress	encounter	enormous	forthcoming
incline	integrity	intrinsic	invoke	levy	likewise
nonetheless	notwithstanding	odd	ongoing	panel	persist
pose	reluctance	so-called	straightforward	undergo	whereby

Adapted from Coxhead (2000)

Resources *(cont.)*

Circle Map

Name _____

Directions: Write the word your teacher tells you to write in the center circle. Think of other words that relate to the word in the center circle. Write your answers in the outer circle.

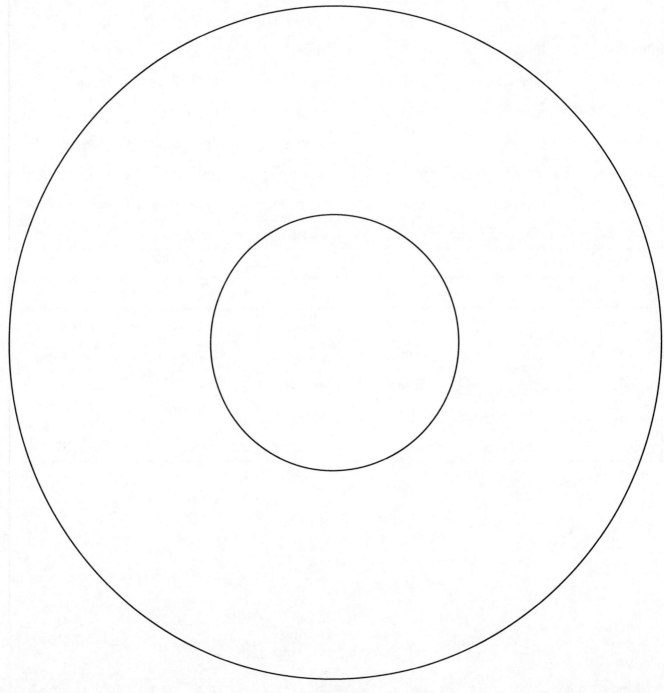

Resources *(cont.)*

• • • • • • • • • • • • • • •

K/W/H/L Chart

Name _____

Directions: Listen to your teacher for the topic you will be studying. Write everything you know about the topic in the *K* column. Write what you want to know about the topic in the *W* column. Write how you plan to find out about your questions in the *H* column. When you are done researching your topic, write what you learned in the *L* column.

K	W	H	L
What We Know	**What We Want to Know**	**How We Will Find Out**	**What We Have Learned**

Resources (cont.)

Word Definition Map

Name

Directions: Listen to your teacher for the vocabulary word. Write the word on the blank lines below. Answer the questions in each column.

What is _____?	What do you know about _____?	What is an example of _____?	What is _____ like?

Resources *(cont.)*

• • • • • • • • • • • • • •

Everyday to Specialized Content

Name _____

Directions: Match the definitions to the vocabulary words below. Decide which meaning is the best specialized content meaning for this unit.

A. _____

B. _____

C. _____

D. _____

E. _____

F. _____

Word	Everyday Meanings	Specialized Content Meanings
_____	_____	_____
	_____	_____
_____	_____	_____
	_____	_____

Directions: Fill in the word that best completes the sentence.

1. _____

2. _____

3. _____

4. _____

106

Comprehensible Input

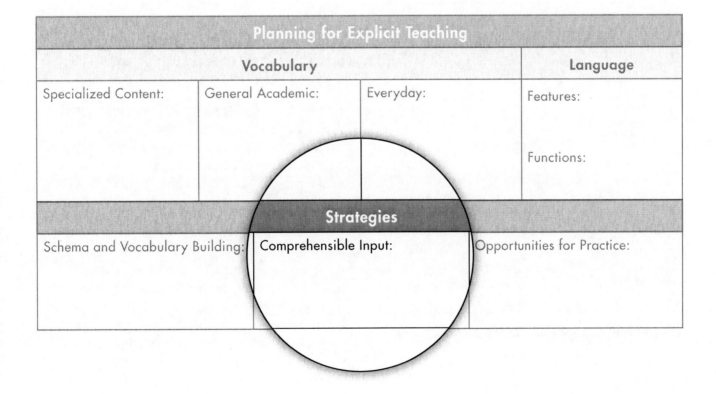

Planning for Explicit Teaching			
Vocabulary			**Language**
Specialized Content:	General Academic:	Everyday:	Features:
			Functions:
Strategies			
Schema and Vocabulary Building:	Comprehensible Input:		Opportunities for Practice:

How Students Benefit

What Is Comprehensible Input?

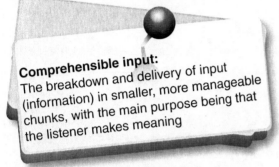

Comprehensible input:
The breakdown and delivery of input (information) in smaller, more manageable chunks, with the main purpose being that the listener makes meaning

In general, comprehensible input in the classroom refers to the ways in which teachers present information so that it is understandable for students, especially English language learners. The processes of breaking down information to make it understandable begins even as we are directing students during a lesson. As fluent speakers of English, many of us forget that the directions we are giving or the words used during the lesson can be confusing to our English language learners.

A quote from de Jong and Harper (2005, 205) highlights this reality:

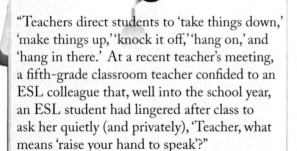

"Teachers direct students to 'take things down,' 'make things up,' 'knock it off,' 'hang on,' and 'hang in there.' At a recent teacher's meeting, a fifth-grade classroom teacher confided to an ESL colleague that, well into the school year, an ESL student had lingered after class to ask her quietly (and privately), 'Teacher, what means 'raise your hand to speak'?'"

Good teachers of English language learners monitor their own language use and that of their students to provide the necessary verbal and nonverbal support structures for classroom participation and learning.

A few ways teachers can make content more comprehensible include simplifying their language use, preteaching vocabulary before the lesson, or using pictures to make a concept more concrete.

Why Should I Use It?

The term *comprehensible input* comes from Krashen's Natural Approach to Second Language Instruction (Krashen 1982; Krashen and Terrell 2000). According to Krashen, to support second-language learning, the teacher's linguistic input should be just slightly above the student's current language development level. Rate of speech, enunciation, complexity of vocabulary, and the use of idiomatic expressions all contribute to the comprehensibility of the teacher's input.

Key to this is that teachers accurately evaluate their students' language proficiency. Teachers may presume that a student has a higher level of understanding of academic content because he or she can communicate competently in social situations.

However, it can take much longer for students to acquire proficiency in academic language. On the other hand, teachers should not assume that just because a student is not speaking much, he or she has limited academic abilities. Some English-learning students have had rich learning experiences in their first language but are unable to communicate these ideas in English. These students might understand much more than they can demonstrate through oral language (de Jong and Harper 2005).

How Students Benefit (cont.)

What Makes Input Comprehensible?

So, what exactly makes input comprehensible? There are two forms of comprehensible input: linguistic and nonlinguistic (Krashen 1982; Krashen and Terrell 2000).

Linguistically, a teacher can aid comprehension in three ways:

- Articulate clearly and slow your rate of speech.

- Use more high-frequency vocabulary and minimize the use of idioms and slang.

- Speak in simpler, shorter sentences.

Nonlinguistic support for English language learners is almost more critical. Nonlinguistic input supports the teacher's verbal presentation of information and can aid comprehension. It can take a variety of forms such as the following:

- graphic organizers

- sentence frames

- realia

- pictures

The strategies in this section support the nonlinguistic aspect and can be found on pages 110–121.

Scaffolding

Designing the proper scaffolds to support student learning goes a long way in making input comprehensible for students. There are many techniques teachers can use to scaffold instruction, but key to making any of them work is the idea that they must gradually be removed. Think of how actual scaffolds are used in construction. Supports are built around and alongside a building or wall while it is being created or worked on. As the work progresses, scaffolds are slowly removed as the new structure can begin to support itself. Upon completion of the building or wall, all the scaffolding is removed. It works the same way for students. When teachers introduce a new concept, they should provide as much support as possible so that students can begin to take hold of the new content rather than crumble under its weight. As students learn more, practice more, and begin to build their concept knowledge, teachers slowly remove some of the support and see how they do. Assuming they are able to stand on their own with the new material, teachers continue to work with them until students reach the point of being able to comprehend and use the content with little to no instructional support—without scaffolds.

Sentence frames are a technique teachers can use to scaffold instruction. A sentence frame is a way to support instruction for students on the features and the functions of language. Teachers can create sentence frames that assist students in expressing functions such as compare and contrast or sequencing. Sentence frames that encourage students to simply use a grammatically correct complete sentence are also important scaffolds that will go a long way in developing students' speaking and writing skills. These sentence frames will likely need to be taught to students in the context of the lesson. Students should be given ample opportunities to use these frames during their lesson practice, which is why this strategy is not only presented in this section (see page 120) but also throughout the Opportunities for Practice section of this book.

The following pages highlight more strategies teachers can use as instructional scaffolds.

Strategies for the Classroom

Supporting the Visual Modality

Overview

There are many strategies teachers can use to make input comprehensible. When selecting strategies there are several things to consider; students' English language proficency level and grade level are just two that may influence the choice of strategies. Consider the different modalities. It is best for English language learners if the lessons are delivered using multiple modes of delivery. The modalities include:

- **visual (learning through the eyes)—using realia, semantic maps, and videos to bring the content to life**

- auditory (learning through the ears)—having students learn information using a chant or through music

- tactile (learning through the hands)—encouraging students to touch realia or use manipulatives to present information

- kinesthetic (learning by moving)—engaging in movement to represent different ideas

Standards

- **McREL:** Students will use level-appropriate vocabulary in speech.

- **TESOL:** Students will use appropriate learning strategies to construct and apply academic knowledge.

Directions

To incorporate this strategy, do the following:

1. Begin by reviewing the content of the text. Think about what visual demonstration would be beneficial to your students. Prior to teaching the lesson, gather any visual support you plan to use.

2. As you teach the lesson, integrate the visual support that you have selected.

A visual demonstration at the start of a new lesson (e.g., graphic organizers, pictures, realia, maps, video) strengthens English language learners' understanding of the concepts being taught.

Differentiating by Proficiency Level

Beginning:	Intermediate:	Advanced:
Using chart paper or a transparency, create a model of the activity you are doing as a class. Complete the activity together, allowing students to see your model as a visual.	Have several pictures pertaining to the topic, and several pictures not pertaining to the topic. Ask students to sort the pictures to see the connection and to enhance comprehension.	After watching a short video relevant to the topic, ask students to write a short summary of what they viewed.

Strategies for the Classroom *(cont.)*

Supporting the Visual Modality *(cont.)*

Below are examples of how this strategy can be incorporated in a lesson.

Grades 1–2

Text Topic: Money

Example: Using bills and coins, students are given the opportunity to examine this realia up close. Students are given the opportunity to notice the details of each one: size, color, decoration, etc.

10¢   25¢

total 35¢

Grades 3–5

Text Topic: Fractions

Example: The teacher compares fractions with a drawing of pizzas as a form of visual representation. Students have a better understanding of fractions when they see two pizzas with different fractions imbedded within each. As a result, they understand the vocabulary word *equivalent*.

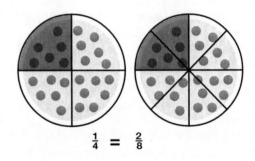

$$\frac{1}{4} = \frac{2}{8}$$

Grades 6–8

Text Topic: Geographic Features of China

Example: While studying the geographic features of China, students are asked to view various video clip sources in order to help bring the topic to life.

Strategies for the Classroom *(cont.)*

Supporting the Auditory Modality

Overview

There are many strategies teachers can use to make input comprehensible. When selecting strategies there are several things to consider: students' English language proficiency level and grade level are just two that may influence the choice of strategies. Consider the different modalities. It is best for English language learners if the lessons are delivered using multiple modes of delivery. The modalities include:

- visual (learning through the eyes)—using realia, semantic maps, and videos to bring the content to life

- **auditory (learning through the ears)—having students learn information using a chant or through music**

- tactile (learning through the hands)—encouraging students to touch realia or use manipulatives to present information

- kinesthetic (learning by moving)—engaging movement to represent different ideas.

Standards

- **McREL:** Students will use level-appropriate vocabulary in speech.

- **TESOL:** Students will use appropriate learning strategies to construct and apply academic knowledge.

Directions

To incorporate this strategy, do the following:

1. Begin by reviewing the content. Think about activity resources related to the topic you might have for students. Think about where you might offer students the opportunity to discuss what they are learning in ways that will help them solidify the learning. Prior to teaching the lesson, gather any support you plan to use.

2. As you teach the lesson, integrate the auditory support that you have selected.

Differentiating by Proficiency Level

Beginning:	Intermediate:	Advanced:
As a front-loading activity, have students listen to a recording of a book or piece of text they will need for the lesson.	Create a short song, chant, or rhyme to capture the main ideas of the lesson. Share this during the lesson as part of your input. Give students several opportunities to practice and repeat the song, chant, or rhyme.	Have students listen to a song, chant, or rhyme. As a summative activity, students might work in groups to create their own song, chant, or rhyme to share with the class.

112

Strategies for the Classroom (cont.)

Supporting the Auditory Modality (cont.)

Below are examples of how this strategy can be incorporated in a lesson.

Grades 1-2

Text Topic: Members of a Community

Example: Students listen to various sounds associated with the roles of members of a community. Some examples for this lesson topic include: fire alarms (firefighters), police sirens (policeman), trash trucks (waste haulers), and a whistle (crossing guards). After listening to the various sounds, students compare and contrast the sounds associated with the members of a community.

Grades 3-5

Text Topic: American Presidents

Example: The teacher plays excerpts of speeches associated with presidents whom students are currently studying. To further support this modality, students are then asked to determine the main ideas that are expressed in the audio clips. For example, after listening to a president's inauguration speech, students analyze the main idea of what an inauguration speech is.

Grades 6-8

Text Topic: Civil War

Example: Students listen to Civil War-era battle hymns and discuss what is being heard. To further support this modality, students are then asked to determine the main ideas that are stated in the audio clips. For example, students listen to various battle hymns and summarize why the Civil War started, who fought in the war, and what the outcome was.

Strategies for the Classroom (cont.)

Supporting the Tactile Modality

Overview

There are many strategies teachers can use to make input comprehensible. When selecting strategies there are several things to consider: students' English language proficiency level and grade level are just two that may influence the choice of strategies. Consider the different modalities. It is best for English language learners if the lessons are delivered using multiple modes of delivery. The modalities include:

- visual (learning through the eyes)—using realia, semantic maps, and videos to bring the content to life

- auditory (learning through the ears)—having students learn information using a chant or through music

- **tactile (learning through the hands)—encouraging students to touch realia or use manipulatives to present information**

- kinesthetic (learning by moving)—engaging movement to represent different ideas

Standards

- **McREL:** Students will ask and respond to questions about the meaning of words.

- **TESOL:** Students will use appropriate learning strategies to construct and apply academic knowledge.

Directions

To incorporate this strategy, do the following:

1. Begin by reviewing the content. Think about realia, objects, or manipulatives you could provide students that would enhance their understanding of the learning. Prior to teaching the lesson, gather any of these items you plan to use.

2. As you teach the lesson, integrate the tactile support that you have selected.

Differentiating by Proficiency Level

Beginning:	Intermediate:	Advanced:
Bring in realia related to the lesson. Encourage students to examine the objects as a front-loading activity.	Bring in realia related to the lesson. After students examine the objects, offer a discussion prompt for speaking about the objects with a partner.	Bring in realia related to the lesson. After students examine and discuss the objects, have them write about the objects in their journal.

Strategies for the Classroom (cont.)

Supporting the Tactile Modality (cont.)

Below are examples of how this strategy can be incorporated in a lesson.

Grades 1–2

Text Topic: Properties of Matter

Example: Students are given an ice cube. As they stand outside, students have the opportunity to physically see and hold their ice cubes as they change from a solid to a liquid.

Grades 3–5

Text Topic: 3-D Geometric Shapes

Example: The teacher provides students with patterns for creating a cube, rectangular prism, cone, and sphere. Students create the geometric shapes and use them as a reference throughout the unit.

Grades 6–8

Text Topic: Earth's Composition

Example: The teacher provides each student with modeling clay in five different colors. As an informal assessment at the beginning of a unit, students are asked to model the layers of Earth's composition (core, mantle, lithosphere, hydrosphere, and atmosphere).

Strategies for the Classroom (cont.)

Supporting the Kinesthetic Modality

Overview

There are many strategies teachers can use to make input comprehensible. When selecting strategies there are several things to consider: students' English language proficiency level and grade level are just two that may influence the choice of strategies. Consider the different modalities. It is best for English language learners if the lessons are delivered using multiple modes of delivery. The modalities include:

- visual (learning through the eyes)— using realia, semantic maps, and videos to bring the content to life

- auditory (learning through the ears)— having students learn information using a chant or through music

- tactile (learning through the hands)— encouraging students to touch realia or use manipulatives to present information

- **kinesthetic (learning by moving)— engaging movement to represent different ideas**

Standards

- **McREL:** Students will ask and respond to questions about the meaning of words.

- **TESOL:** Students will use appropriate learning strategies to construct and apply academic knowledge.

Directions

To incorporate this strategy, do the following:

1. Begin by reviewing the content. Think about where you could provide students opportunities for movement that would enhance their understanding of the learning. Prior to teaching the lesson, gather any support you plan to use.

2. As you teach the lesson, integrate the kinesthetic support that you have selected to use.

Differentiating by Proficiency Level

Beginning:	Intermediate:	Advanced:
Create movements associated with the content. Have students practice the movements to reinforce their concept building.	Have students watch the demonstration of a movement associated with a concept they are learning and ask them to create a movement of their own.	Have students create their own movements associated with a learned concept, then present it to the class, explaining and teaching others their movement.

Strategies for the Classroom (cont.)

Supporting the Kinesthetic Modality (cont.)

Below are examples of how this strategy can be incorporated in a lesson.

Grades 1-2

Text Topic: Clouds

Example: Using their hands, students incorporate the kinesthetic modality by depicting the different shapes of clouds. For example, a cirrocumulus cloud is depicted by pretending to fluff a pillow.

Grades 3-5

Text Topic: Plants

Example: The growth of a plant is depicted by using the kinesthetic modality. Students are asked to use their bodies to represent the cycle of a plant from seed to adult, such as curling up in a ball (seed) to stretching out (adult).

Grades 6-8

Text Topic: Plate Tectonics

Example: Plate tectonics is depicted by engaging movement to represent the different parts of the Earth. Many scientists believe that the ridges represent areas where new crust is being formed as hot magma escapes from Earth's core. Students are asked to incorporate the kinesthetic modality to represent this information. Students place their hands in an upward position and wiggle towards the sky (hot magma escaping). The crust is depicted with the other hand blocking the magma from escaping.

Strategies for the Classroom (cont.)

Study Guides

Overview

To make the content area textbook more comprehensible, teachers can use Study Guides. This strategy helps highlight key concepts and vocabulary. Study Guides are a way to support students while they read a textbook that is above their instructional reading level. Study Guides can be written differently for different students, based on their needs and may include brief summaries of important sections in the text and include questions for readers to think about or write down. This strategy can extend or enrich the content being presented for students who are able to read the text easily.

Standards

- **McREL:** Students will understand level-appropriate reading vocabulary.

- **TESOL:** Students will use appropriate learning strategies to construct and apply academic knowledge.

Directions

To incorporate this strategy do the following:

1. Preread the piece of text students will read during the lesson.

2. Identify a few main ideas and details students will need to recognize in order to comprehend the text.

3. Design questions that will help students elicit those important ideas from the text.

4. Include quick tasks such as summarizing or illustrating a concept that can aid in comprehension.

5. Modify questions or tasks based on students' needs to design several different study guides for the same text.

Differentiating by Proficiency Level

Beginning:
Create a more simplistic study guide integrating pictures representing the content of the lesson.

Intermediate:
Include a short written summary of important concepts in the text written in language accessible to intermediate level learners.

Advanced:
Have students create their own questions to share with classmates. Encourage students to ask their questions.

       118

Strategies for the Classroom (cont.)

Study Guides (cont.)

Below are examples of how this strategy can be incorporated in a lesson.

Grades 1–2

Patterns
➡ This is an ABAB pattern.
△ ○ △ ○ △ ○
➡ This is an ABBA pattern.
△ ○ ○ △ ○ ○ △

Text Topic: Patterns

Example: Prior to teaching the lesson, the teacher notices that students will have to solve a mathematical word problem pertaining to patterns in a garden. The teacher creates the following questions to ask students: *How can you tell the flowers form an ABBA pattern? What are some other patterns that will need to be planted in the gardens?* During the lesson, as students respond to the questions, the teacher illustrates the pattern on the board to aid in comprehension and distributes a study guide to students that consists of a worksheet created by the teacher depicting the pattern addressed in the text.

Grades 3–5

Text Topic: Division

Example: Prior to teaching the lesson, the teacher notices that students will have to solve mathematical problems pertaining to division. The teacher creates the following questions: *How many do you currently have? Into how many parts should it be divided?* Students write the questions on a sheet of paper as a reminder and a study guide of the questions they must answer to help solve the questions.

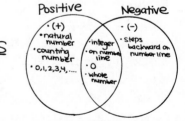

Integers

Grades 6–8

Text Topic: Positive and Negative Integers

Example: Prior to teaching the lesson, the teacher notices that students will have to solve a mathematical problem pertaining to positive and negative integers. The teacher creates the following questions: *What are the similiarities between positive and negative integers? What are the differences?* During the lesson as students respond to the questions, the teacher creates a Venn diagram as a study guide.

Strategies for the Classroom (cont.)

Sentence Frames

Overview

A sentence frame is a way to support instruction for students on the features of language (grammar and sentence structure) while also incorporating the functions of language (cognitive structures). In their writing and speaking, students need to combine sentences to formulate complex thoughts and correctly use conjunctions, prepositions, idiomatic expressions, and other grammatical phrasing in order to be considered academically literate. By using a sentence frame, teachers provide students with a scaffold for both their thinking and speaking.

Standards

- **McREL:** Students will understand level-appropriate sight words and vocabulary.

- **TESOL:** Students will use English to obtain, process, construct, and provide subject matter information in spoken and written form.

Directions

To incorporate this strategy, do the following:

1. Consider the purpose of the language students should produce (e.g., expressing fact and opinion, defining a term).

2. Write a frame (or a series of frames) that provides students a stem and structure for their speaking and/or writing.

Differentiating by Proficiency Level

Beginning:
Sentence frames should be fairly simple for beginning English language learners. If delivering a lesson on classifying and categorizing, the frame that can be used is _____ and _____ are types of _____.

Intermediate:
At this level, sentence frames can integrate complex language that can require students to provide more information. Continuing the example for classifying and categorizing, a frame appropriate for intermediate students might be: _____, _____, and _____ are all examples of _____.

Advanced:
Advanced students can be provided frames that include even more complex syntax and require more input from students. Following the classifying and categorizing example, _____ and _____ have/are both _____, so we can categorize them as _____ would be an appropriate frame.

Strategies for the Classroom (cont.)

Sentence Frames (cont.)

Below are examples of how this strategy can be incorporated in a lesson.

Grades 1–2

Text Topic: Planets (with focus on cause and effect language function)

Example:

Science Text: *Earth is our planet. It is the best planet for life. Mars is called the red planet. That is because the soil on Mars is red.*

Sentence Frame: _____ *is called the red planet because* _____.

Grades 3–5

Text Topic: Simple Machines (with focus on compare and contrast language function)

Example:

Science Text: *An inclined plane is a slanted surface. It is easier to use force to move an object along the slanted surface than it is to lift and move it. A pulley is a wheel that is attached to a frame. When force is used to pull on one end of the rope, the object is raised.*

Sentence Frames: _____ *and* _____ *are similar because they both* _____.
_____ *and* _____ *are different in that* _____.

Grades 6–8

Text Topic: Distributive Property (with focus on sequencing language function)

Example:

Mathematics Text: Solve the following for x: $4(6 + 2x)$.

Sentence Frames: *The* _____ *property can be applied here because* _____.
First, _____. *Then,* _____. *Next,* _____. *Finally,* _____.

Resources

· · · · · · · · · · ·

Classify and Categorize

Frame	Example
"There are _____ types/kinds of _____." "_____, _____, and _____ are all/all have _____." "_____ and _____ could be classified as _____ because _____." "Because _____ are all/all have _____, we could categorize them as _____."	There are three general types of clouds. Stratus, cumulus, and cirrus are all types of clouds. Cumulonimbus and nimbostratus could be classified as low clouds because they appear below three kilometers. Because cirrostratus, cirrus, and cirrocumulus clouds are all found above nine kilometers, we could categorize them as high clouds.

Cause and Effect

Frame	Example
"_____ because _____." "Because/Since _____ is/was _____, _____." "As a result of _____, _____."	The ice melted because it was hot outside. Since the weather was hot, all of the ice melted. As a result of the warm weather, the ice melted.

Resources (cont.)

· · · · · · · · · · · · · ·

Compare and Contrast

Frame	Example
"A _____ is/has _____, but a _____ is/has _____."	A blizzard has snow, but a northeaster has snow or rain.
"They both are/have _____, but a _____ is/has _____."	They both are storms, but a northeaster is a snowstorm or a rainstorm.
"_____ and _____ are similar/different because _____."	A blizzard and a northeaster are similar because they can both produce significant snowfall.
"There are many similarities/differences between _____ and _____. For example, they both _____." Or, "There are many differences between _____ and _____. For example, _____ but _____."	There are many differences between a blizzard and a northeaster. For example, blizzards are characterized by extremely low temperatures but northeasters can occur in very cold or somewhat warm temperatures.

Sequencing

Frame	Example
"First, _____. Then, _____. Next, _____. Finally, _____."	First, mix the dry ingredients in a large bowl. Then, combine the wet ingredients in a separate bowl. Next, add the wet ingredients to the dry and stir. Finally, pour the mixture into the cake pan.
"To begin, _____."	To begin, you need a clean, dry space in which to work.
"Prior to _____, _____."	Prior to baking the cake, you need to purchase all of your ingredients.
"Lastly, _____."	Lastly, put the cake in the oven and bake at 375 degrees.
"Once you _____, then you _____."	Once you have combined all of the ingredients, then you pour the mixture into the cake pan.

Resources (cont.)

Main Idea

Frame	Example
"It is mainly about _____."	It is mainly about the ways alligators and crocodiles are alike and different.
"The main idea is _____. "	The main idea is the similarities and differences between alligators and crocodiles.
"The main idea is _____. A detail that supports this is _____."	The main idea is the similarities and differences between alligators and crocodiles. A detail that supports this is that alligators and crocodiles both have a long fourth tooth.

Fact and Opinion

Frame	Example
"_____ is a fact because _____."	George Washington was the first president is a fact because we can prove it.
"_____ is an opinion because we cannot prove _____."	George Washington was a brave man is an opinion because we cannot prove that everyone agrees he was brave.
"The word _____ is evidence that this statement is a(n)_____ because _____."	The word *brave* is evidence that this statement is an opinion because it explains what someone thinks about George Washington.

124

Resources (cont.)

Signal Words

Signal Words for Cause		
because	bring about	contributed to
due to	the reason for	give rise to
led to	on account of	created by
since	given that	while
as	whereas	as a result of

Signal Words for Effect		
as a result	consequently	hence
so	therefore	for this reason
outcome	finally	then
after	accordingly	subsequently

Signal Words for Comparing		
like	similar	as
same	in the same way	too
both	most important	have in common
the same as	similarly	as well as

Signal Words for Contrast		
although	yet	whereas
however	but	while
differ	instead	unless
unlike	on the contrary	contrary to
even though	on the other hand	the reverse

Resources *(cont.)*

• • • • • • • • • • • • • • • •

Signal Words

Signal Words for Classify and Categorize		
Categories	elements	numbers
characteristics	features	parts
classes	groups	sorts
classify	kinds	types
divide	methods	ways
dimensions	aspects	

Signal Words for Sequencing		
first	then	next
last	second	third
before	afterward	as soon as
eventually	meanwhile	finally
later	after	while
during	subsequently	now

Signal Words for Fact		
is	are	have
was	were	will be

Signal Words for Opinion		
believe	think	seems
may	appears	probably
likely	possibly	feel
good	bad	best
excellent	awful	greatest

Signal Words for Summarize (Main Idea)		
accordingly	last of all	basically
to summarize	consequently	therefore
finally	the effect	hence
the implication	in conclusion	the most important
in retrospect	thus	in summary
to recapitulate	then	as a result
last of all	in brief	in short
on the whole	to sum up	ultimately

126

Resources *(cont.)*

● ● ● ● ● ● ● ● ● ● ● ● ● ● ● ●

Graphic Organizer for Comparing and Contrasting

Name _____

Directions: In the left side of the rectangle, write 2–3 things about Topic 1. In the right side of the rectangle, write 2–3 things about Topic 2. In the bottom half of the triangle, write 2–3 things about Topic 3. In the area where all three shapes come together, write one thing that is common to all three topics.

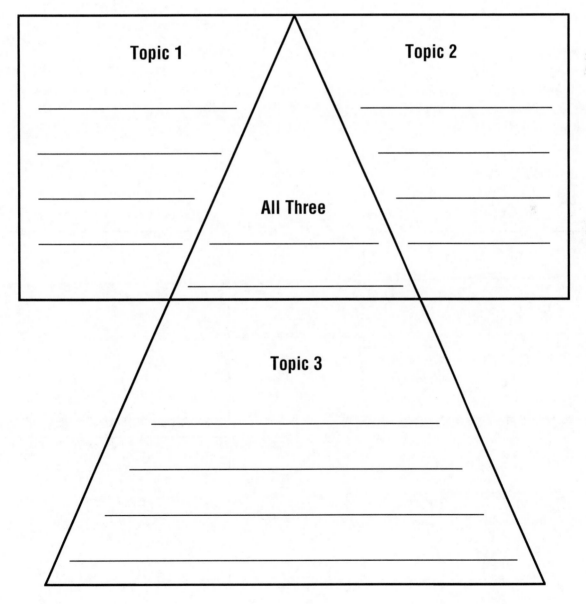

Resources (cont.)

• • • • • • • • • • • • • • •

Graphic Organizer for Cause and Effect

Name _____

Directions: Choose one event that caused many other events to happen and write it in the box labeled *Cause*. Then write the effects in the other boxes.

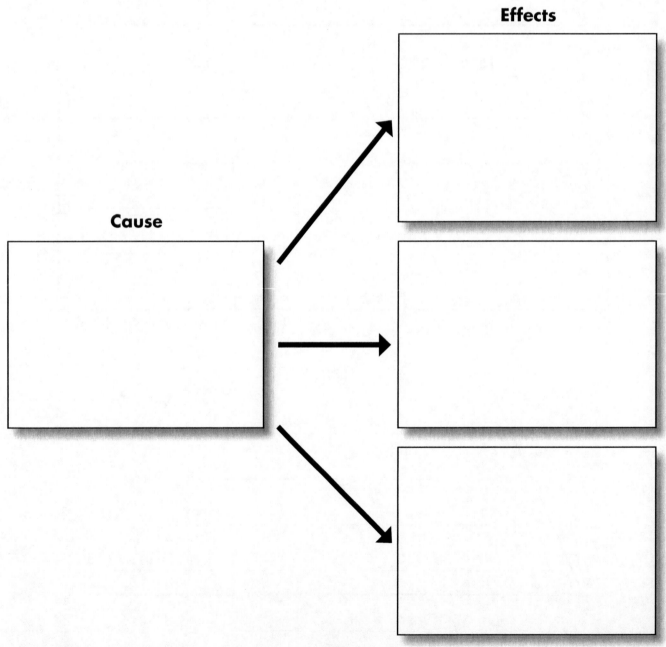

Resources *(cont.)*

• • • • • • • • • • • • • • •

Graphic Organizer for Classifying and Categorizing

Name _____

Directions: Write in the topic. Then make a list of words about the topic. Look at the list and create categories of related words. Be sure to label each category.

Topic: _____

List

_____   _____   _____

_____   _____   _____

_____   _____   _____

_____   _____   _____

_____   _____   _____

_____   _____   _____

Categories

_____   _____   _____

_____   _____   _____

_____   _____   _____

_____   _____   _____

_____   _____   _____

Resources (cont.)

Graphic Organizer for Sequencing

Name _____

Directions: Think about the text you read. Write the beginning, the middle, and the end.

Beginning:

_____

_____

_____

Middle:

_____

_____

_____

End:

_____

_____

_____

Resources (cont.)

Graphic Organizer for Main Ideas

Name _____

Directions: Write the passage from the text in the large rectangle. Read through the passage. Write the main idea in the second rectangle. Then make a list of important points in the passage. Write your summary in 20 words or less.

Passage

_____

_____

_____

_____

Main Idea

_____

Important Points

_____	_____
_____	_____
_____	_____

Summary

_____

_____

Resources

Graphic Organizer for Fact and Opinion

Name _____

Directions: Complete the table below. Record your findings as *fact* or *opinion* and explain why it is a fact or opinion.

Fact	Opinion	Why?		

Opportunities for Practice

Planning for Explicit Teaching			
Vocabulary			**Language**
Specialized Content:	General Academic:	Everyday:	Features:
			Functions:
Strategies			
Schema and Vocabulary Building:	Comprehensible Input:		Opportunities for Practice:

How Students Benefit

What Are Opportunities for Practice?

While we are providing students explicit instruction in academic language during content-area instruction, we need to make sure they also get multiple opportunities to practice the language skills that they are learning. Research shows that when students practice production, they move from attending to semantic processing (meaning) to syntactic processing (forms and features) of the new language. In other words, they move from expressing the gist of something to focusing on properly expressing those ideas in the new language. Students pay attention to correct usage of grammatical features, verb tense, sentence structure, and vocabulary—all markers of proficiency in academic language.

Opportunities for practice should be through authentic, structured activities that allow students to produce both written and spoken products. The more students practice, the more likely that academic language will become part of their repertoire.

Oral Practice

While comprehensible input has been shown to facilitate language acquisition, what about the opportunity to use that information? Lesson planning naturally includes some sort of practice or activity for students that will allow them to use new information, but how often does that include oral practice? Are we comfortable with letting students talk during a lesson?

The works of Swain (1985), Scarcella (2003), and Scarcella, Anderson and Krashen (1991) examine the need for students to produce and practice new language skills in order to achieve academic literacy. In short, students need to do something with the input they receive.

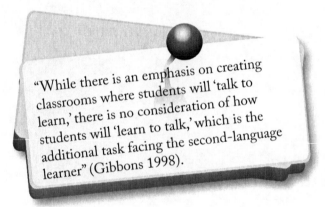

"While there is an emphasis on creating classrooms where students will 'talk to learn,' there is no consideration of how students will 'learn to talk,' which is the additional task facing the second-language learner" (Gibbons 1998).

How Students Benefit (cont.)

Active Participation Strategies

Much of the research on second-language acquisition supports the idea of using a variety of active participation strategies. Active participation strategies can serve the dual purpose of keeping students engaged throughout the lesson (which is essential with learning the material) and providing opportunities for both oral and written practice through small-group interactions. These strategies can be easily applied to any content-area instruction and adapted to any grade level.

Many of these active participation strategies require students to participate in a discussion that extends beyond a typical call-and-response interaction between the teacher and student. When used effectively during content-area instruction, this active format allows students to explore and manipulate the language of the discipline in a low-stress environment (since they are paired or grouped with peers) and in an environment in which they receive feedback from classmates. These strategies are particularly powerful if English language learners have the opportunity to practice with Standard English Speaking (SES) peers. Many of these strategies are developed from the research by Kagan (1989), Slavin (1989), and Johnson and Johnson (1986) in relation to cooperative learning.

The following pages describe several active participation strategies teachers can use to facilitate opportunities for practice in any content-area lesson.

Strategies for the Classroom

Think-Pair-Share

Overview

This strategy involves the teacher providing a prompt or question. Students are then given time to think of a response and then discuss it with a partner. The teacher then provides a way for students to share with the larger group. Effective use of Think-Pair-Share provides students with the opportunity to use academic language in a low-stress environment because they get to practice with a peer before sharing with the class.

Standards

- **McREL:** Students will use level-appropriate vocabulary in speech.

- **TESOL:** Students will use English to obtain, process, construct, and provide subject matter information in spoken and written form.

Directions

To incorporate this strategy, do the following:

1. After prompting students, allow a brief, silent wait time for students to individually formulate their responses. For English language learners, this is particularly essential in generating the language required for a response.

2. Circulate around the room and listen to student discussions. This allows the opportunity to provide direction and corrective feedback, if necessary, or to clarify student understanding of content and use of academic language.

3. Encourage students to share their discussions with the class.

This strategy provides oral language practice, but can also be adapted to provide a combination of oral and written practice. This is commonly referred to as a *Think-Write-Pair-Share*. Students are asked to write what they have thought about before they discuss their ideas with their partner (see page 160).

Differentiating by Proficiency Level

Beginning:	Intermediate:	Advanced:
Have students think about the question integrating a simple sentence frame (see page 120). Then have students share their answer with a partner before sharing with the class.	Integrate a sentence frame (see page 120) more complex for students at this level. Then have students share their answer with a partner before sharing with the class.	Integrate a sentence frame (see page 120) requiring critical thinking skills for students at this level. Then have students share their answer with a partner before sharing with the class.

Strategies for the Classroom (cont.)

Think-Pair-Share (cont.)

Below are examples of how this strategy can be incorporated in a lesson.

Grades 1–2

Text Topic: My Community

Example: While reading a passage about different jobs in the community, the teacher stops and asks students the following questions: *What are some jobs you have seen in our community? What do people need to know to do these jobs?* With each question that is asked, students think about an answer, find a partner, and share their answer. The teacher then selects student volunteers to share some responses.

Grades 3–5

Text Topic: Maps

Example: Students are learning how to read maps. *Symbol* and *legend* are key vocabulary words for this lesson, so the teacher prompts students to use their vocabulary words during a discussion with partners. The teacher stops and asks students the following questions: *What are some symbols you might see on a map? What do these symbols mean?* With each question that is asked, students think about an answer, find a partner and share their answer. The teacher then selects student volunteers to share some responses.

Grades 6–8

Text Topic: American Revolution

Example: Students are independently reading a social studies passage. The teacher wants students to summarize their reading in a short discussion with a partner while building their concept knowledge on the vocabulary word *loyalist*. The teacher asks students the following question: *What could be some of the reasons the loyalists continued to pledge their allegiance to the king?* Students think about an answer, find a partner, and share their answer. The teacher then selects student volunteers to share some responses.

Strategies for the Classroom (cont.)

Talking Chips

Overview

This strategy ensures that everyone has an opportunity to share in a discussion. Once the teacher has provided a prompt, students take turns participating in the conversation by throwing in their talking chip. This strategy provides students with the opportunity to use academic language in a low-stress environment because they get to hear the proper usage of academic language from language models.

Standards

- **McREL:** Students will use level-appropriate vocabulary in speech.

- **TESOL:** Students will use English to obtain, process, construct, and provide subject matter information in spoken and written form.

Directions

To incorporate this strategy, do the following:

1. Before the lesson, assign students to discussion groups and give each student a designated number of chips to use during the discussion (see page 161).

2. Ask a question or provide a prompt to the groups and give students time to gather their thoughts and record some of their ideas.

3. Tell students that there is a minimum number of chips they must use during the discussion. For example, if each student has two chips, the teacher may request that each person use at least one chip during the discussion. This means that each person in the group must contribute at least once to the discussion.

4. As students discuss, they place a chip in the center of the table when it is their turn to speak. The teacher should circulate around the room to monitor discussions. When it seems that everyone has contributed at least one chip, signal the end of the discussion period.

Differentiating by Proficiency Level

Beginning:	Intermediate:	Advanced:
Give students picture vocabulary cards and a few sentence frames (see page 120) to help them with the discussion.	Provide some complex sentence frames (see page 120) to encourage complex responses.	Ask students to paraphrase what the person before them said and expand or reflect on his or her statements.

Strategies for the Classroom (cont.)

Talking Chips (cont.)

Below are examples of how this strategy can be incorporated in a lesson.

Grades 1–2

Text Topic: Weather

Example: To activate prior knowledge before a unit on weather, the teacher arranges students in small groups of four or five. Each group is given a set of picture cards that depict different weather conditions (e.g., hail, drizzle, blizzard, humidity, hurricane) and represents some of the unit vocabulary. Each group is directed to use their talking chips to discuss what they know about each weather condition. Students use the picture cards as clues and every time they speak they turn in a chip.

Grades 3–5

Text Topic: Main Character Analysis

Example: After working together as a class to create a Venn diagram comparing and contrasting the main characters from two stories the class read during the week, the teacher arranges students in small groups of four or five. Students use their chips to participate in a discussion of the ways in which the two main characters are alike and different. Some students note the similarities of the characters' personalities. Other students discuss how the characters' behavior in the story is different. Every time a student speaks, a talking chip is turned in. The Venn diagram serves as a "cheat sheet" while students make statements using the academic language of compare and contrast.

Grades 6–8

Text Topic: Persuasive Writing

Example: As a prewriting activity, students are arranged in small groups and asked to use their chips to discuss the general characteristics of persuasive writing. Students share that persuasive writing includes a stated position or belief, factual supports, a logical argument, and a call to action. Every time a student speaks, a talking chip is turned in.

Strategies for the Classroom (cont.)

Not Taboo

Overview

This strategy encourages students to use the vocabulary words during whole-class or small-group interactions. This strategy provides students with the opportunity to use academic language in a low-stress environment because they get to hear the proper usage of academic language from language models.

Standards

- **McREL:** Students will use level-appropriate vocabulary in speech.

- **TESOL:** Students will use English to obtain, process, construct, and provide subject matter information in spoken and written form.

Directions

To incorporate this strategy, do the following:

1. As students begin the lesson, distribute 10 game chips (see page 162).

2. Identify the vocabulary words that students should practice throughout the lesson. These can be words from the unit, words that are being introduced that day, or any words that the class has recently studied. Tell students that they should try to use these words as much as possible, both orally and in writing, as they ask and answer questions or have discussions.

3. Every time the teacher or a classmate observes someone using the word correctly and in context, he or she turns in one of his or her chips.

4. At the end of the lesson, students with the fewest chips left are the "winners."

Differentiating by Proficiency Level

Beginning:
Provide students with specific examples of each vocabulary word and display pictures representing the vocabulary words to help improve comprehension.

Intermediate:
Provide students with index cards with specific vocabulary words written on them. Tell students to keep these words and hold them up when they hear the word being used. They may turn in one of their chips for recognizing the word being used correctly.

Advanced:
Provide students with index cards with specific vocabulary words on them. Ask students to write their own definitions on each card. Each time he or she uses a word correctly, they can turn in a chip.

Strategies for the Classroom (cont.)

Not Taboo (cont.)

Below are examples of how this strategy can be incorporated in a lesson.

Grades 1-2

Text Topic: Telling Time

Example: Students are introduced to the following mathematics vocabulary: *time*, *hour*, *half-hour*, *minute*, and *second*. Students are then encouraged to use these words and listen to classmates using these words throughout the lesson. The teacher creates the opportunity for students to use these words by asking questions or sharing a comment about time strategically throughout the day. For example, a student shares "In a *half-hour* it will be recess time." That student then turns in a chip for using a vocabulary word correctly.

Grades 3-5

Text Topic: Ecosystems

Example: Students are intoduced to the following science vocabulary: *environment*, *consumer*, *producer*, and *reproduce*. Students are then encouraged to use these words and listen to classmates using these words throughout the lesson. For example, while pair-sharing a student comments on the proper use of the word *producer* by his partner. He agrees that an example of a producer is a plant. The partner then turns in a chip for using a vocabulary word correctly.

Grades 6-8

Text Topic: Algebraic Proofs

Example: Students are given the following mathematics vocabulary: *slope*, *parallel*, and *perpendicular*. Students are encouraged to use these words and listen for others using these words throughout the lesson. For example, while sharing the similarities between two angles, a student states that the lines are *parallel*. That student then turns in a chip for using a vocabulary word correctly.

Strategies for the Classroom (cont.)

Whip-Around

Overview

During this strategy, the teacher asks as many students as possible to share a quick response in a brief amount of time. This allows many students to participate at once. This is beneficial from a language perspective because it gives students the opportunity to hear each other use and produce language in response to a question or prompt.

Standards

- **McREL:** Students will use level-appropriate vocabulary in speech.

- **TESOL:** Students will use learning strategies to extend their communicative competence.

Directions

To incorporate this strategy, do the following:

1. Pose a question, prompt, or brief task and give students time to generate their responses. This may involve simply thinking of an oral response or even writing down a few possible responses.

2. "Whip" around the room quickly, having students share their responses. It is important to choose a structured way to whip around the room so that students are ready to respond and a quick pace can be maintained. Examples include: moving up and down rows, clockwise around the room, from table to table, front to back, or back to front of the room.

Differentiating by Proficiency Level

Beginning:	**Intermediate:**	**Advanced:**
Encourage students to answer with simple one- or two-word responses.	Help students prepare a quick written response or two for them to refer to when the Whip-Around reaches them.	Have students write down some of their possible responses to the prompt so that they are prepared to respond when it is their turn.

142

Strategies for the Classroom *(cont.)*

Whip-Around *(cont.)*

Below are examples of how this strategy can be incorporated in a lesson.

Grades 1–2

Text Topic: Money

Example: To close the day's lesson on money, the teacher asks students to think about everything they know about it. The teacher refers students to the posted list of vocabulary for the unit and encourages them to use the words in their response. A student responds with, "*Coins* are a type of *money.*" Another student says, "*Money* is used to *purchase* food."

Grades 3–5

Text Topic: Animals

Example: To activate students' prior knowledge for a science lesson, the teacher refers students to the vocabulary from the previous lesson: *vertebrate, invertebrate, reptile, amphibian,* and *mammal.* Students are directed to use one of the vocabulary words by providing an example of an animal that fits the ascribed category. A student shares, "A worm is an *invertebrate* because it does not have a backbone." Students quickly share their responses during the Whip-Around activity.

Grades 6–8

Text Topic: Civil War

Example: To review for a unit exam on the Civil War, the teacher refers students to the following vocabulary words: *confederacy, regiment, succession,* and *slavery.* Students are given a few minutes to use the words correctly in context, using their notes and vocabulary practice as references. A student shares, "A military division was known as a *regiment.*" Students quickly share their responses during the Whip-Around activity.

Strategies for the Classroom *(cont.)*

Mix-Freeze-Match

Overview

This strategy allows students to mingle around the room waiting for the teacher's signal to stop and exchange an answer or piece of information with a partner. This strategy helps students practice orally using academic language within their responses.

Standards

- **McREL:** Students will use level-appropriate vocabulary in speech.

- **TESOL:** Students will use learning strategies to extend their communicative competence.

Directions

To incorporate this strategy, do the following:

1. Decide what the purpose of the activity will be. For example, perhaps you want students to practice explaining the meaning of their vocabulary words. Prior to the lesson, prepare index cards with the selected vocabulary words, question, or prompt written on each card (see page 163).

2. Distribute an index card to each student. When students receive their card, give them a few moments to formulate a response on what they will be sharing.

3. Tell students to "mix" about the room, waiting for the teacher's signal to "freeze." Give students the signal to freeze and have them "match" with the person nearest to them. Students should have an opportunity to share their answer/information with their partner.

4. Walk around the classroom and listen to students' answers. Repeat the Mix-Freeze-Match cycle as appropriate. Students should match with a different partner each time.

Differentiating by Proficiency Level

Beginning:	Intermediate:	Advanced:
Give students a card with a vocabulary term and an example of the word being used correctly. Students will be able to share the sentence that is written on their card and practice giving an oral answer.	Give students a card with a vocabulary word and a sentence frame (see page 120) on the back that describes the meaning. Students can be given a few minutes to think about how to complete the frame.	Give students a card with a vocabulary word and have them write its meaning, using their own words.

Strategies for the Classroom (cont.)

Mix-Freeze-Match (cont.)

Below are examples of how this strategy can be incorporated in a lesson.

Grades 1–2

Text Topic: Reading Comprehension

Example: After reading a story, students are given picture cards that represent vocabulary words associated with the story. During the Mix-Freeze-Match activity, students are asked to name the word being described in the picture held by their partner. For example, a student shares with a partner a card of a castle and the word *fantasy* printed under the picture. The student tells the partner that the genre of the story was *fantasy*.

Grades 3–5

Text Topic: Factors

Example: As a review to a unit, students are given cards with math terms that have multiple meanings. The back of each card shows the word used in a sentence to illustrate just one of its various meanings. As students participate in Mix-Freeze-Match, they explain the meaning of the word to their partners. An example is the word *factor* and the following sentence: *The factors of 12 are 1, 2, 3, 4, 6, and 12 because those numbers can be evenly divided into 12.*

Grades 6–8

Text Topic: Sentence Combination

Example: Students are given a card with two sentences to combine on one side and a conjunction from the academic word list on the other. For example, *(1) Sheila reads very well. (2) Sheila reads very slowly.* Conjunction: *albeit.* Possible combination: *Shelia reads very well, albeit very slowly.* Students combine the sentences using the conjunction. When students match with a partner, they share their sentence combinations.

Strategies for the Classroom (cont.)

Give and Take

Overview

This strategy provides students with an opportunity to share a piece of information relating to the unit of study (give) in exchange for more information (take). This strategy helps students practice orally using academic language within their responses.

Standards

- **McREL:** Students will use level-appropriate vocabulary in speech.

- **TESOL:** Students will use English to obtain, process, construct, and provide subject matter information in spoken and written form.

Directions

To incorporate this strategy, do the following:

1. Assign a topic or pose a question and have students brainstorm what they know about the topic. Students should write their responses on a sheet of paper (see page 164).

2. Tell students to take their sheet of paper with them as they mingle around the room. At your signal, students walk around the room to choose a partner they want to share with. Give students a few minutes to share what they had written down with their partner.

3. As they discuss the topic, each student should write down any new ideas or information they learned from their partner. Students should be encouraged to discuss the topic with one another, pose questions that clarify, or ask one another to expand on an idea or thought. Encourage students to practice using academic language as they circulate and listen to discussions.

4. When the time for sharing ideas concludes, bring the class together for a whole-class debrief.

Differentiating by Proficiency Level

Beginning:	Intermediate:	Advanced:
Create a poster or a summary sheet that expresses the students' knowledge in simple, complete sentences.	Before the class debriefs, encourage students to use sentence frames (see page 120) to rewrite their thoughts and findings into complete sentences to share.	Have students summarize their learning by defending and supporting their responses as well as their partner's choices.

Strategies for the Classroom (cont.)

Give and Take (cont.)

Below are examples of how this strategy can be incorporated in a lesson.

Grades 1–2

Text Topic: Seasons

Example: The teacher gives students a sheet of paper divided into four boxes, each titled with the name of a season. Each student is assigned a particular season and asked to write or draw something in the box. For example, a student assigned the winter season writes that the winter season is cold and that in several places it snows. At the teacher's signal, students find a partner who had a different season and discuss what they wrote or drew about the season. After a few minutes the class shares their responses and each student takes information that was discussed and completes the activity.

Grades 3–5

Text Topic: Poetry

Example: As an activity to begin a unit on poetry, students are asked to write down what they already know or have learned about poems, poets, or any aspect of poetry. During the Give and Take, students add to their list as they discuss poetry with a partner. For example, a student shares with a partner that poetry can use personification. Since the partner did not have that information, he writes it in the "take" category of his paper. The class then returns to debrief and share aloud what they have learned. This allows other students to write additional notes to what is discussed regarding poetry.

Grades 6–8

Text Topic: Persuasive Writing

Example: Students are given the following topic: *Students should always be given homework on the weekends.* The teacher asks students to take a position for or against the idea. They are then directed to meet with one person who agrees with them and someone who disagrees and do a Give and Take on their reasoning. Before the whole-class debrief, students are given time to summarize what they have learned and what they will share with the class. As an extension to the activity, students write a persuasive essay based on the notes they gathered.

Strategies for the Classroom (cont.)

Inside/Outside Circles

Overview

This strategy requires students to form an inner and outer circle and rotate at the teacher's signal. At each rotation students exchange information based on the prompt or question presented to them. This strategy provides students with the opportunity to practice oral language.

Standards

- **McREL:** Students will use level-appropriate vocabulary in speech.

- **TESOL:** Students will use English to obtain, process, construct, and provide subject matter information in spoken and written form.

Directions

To incorporate this strategy, do the following:

1. Arrange the class into two equal groups. Number off each group and designate one group as the Inside Circle and the other as the Outside Circle.

2. Direct the Inside Circle to form a circle so that they are facing out. Ask the Outside Circle to form a circle around this group so that each student is paired with another. Pairs should be facing each other.

3. Inform students of the prompt they are to discuss or question they are to answer. The teacher can request that both partners discuss or direct a question toward either of the circles. Once partners have discussed their answers, direct one of the circles to move. For example, the Inside Circle could move to the left.

4. Once students move, they should be facing a new partner and ready for the next practice. During this strategy, teachers can encourage the use of vocabulary and academic language as students discuss the prompts or answer the various questions.

Differentiating by Proficiency Level

Beginning:	Intermediate:	Advanced:
Give students a set of prepared answers or statements they can share during this activity.	Provide students sentence frames (see page 120) to reference during the activity, if needed.	Provide a list of potential sentence starters for students to use as a reference during the activity.

Strategies for the Classroom (cont.)

Inside/Outside Circles (cont.)

Below are examples of how this strategy can be incorporated in a lesson.

Grades 1–2

Text Topic: Inferencing

Example: As students stand in their circles, the teacher holds pictures for students to look at. Beneath each picture is a sentence frame for students to use when they respond to their partner. The teacher holds up a picture of a child frowning with the frame *This boy is _____. I think this because _____.* The teacher then says, "All of the students in the Inside Circle, I would like you to look at this picture and use this sentence to tell your partner how you think this boy is feeling." Students in the Inside Circle respond. The teacher then directs the Inside Circle to move one person to their left. The teacher holds up a different picture and says, "Now, students on the outside, it is your turn."

Grades 3–5

Text Topic: Plants

Example: Students are given the following list of terms, which includes both specialized content and general academic vocabulary for the topic: *photosynthesis, sun, fuel, convert, produce, plants, process, energy,* and *chlorophyll.* Students use these words in their responses to review questions on the unit during Inside/Outside Circle. For example, students are asked to describe the role of the sun in photosynthesis. A student responds by saying, "The *sun* provides *energy* for *plants* to use during *photosynthesis.*"

Grades 6–8

Text Topic: Cell Biology

Example: Students are given the following list of terms, which includes both specialized content and general academic vocabulary for the topic: *nucleus, cytoplasm, mitochondrion, cell membrane, tissue, vacuole, cell wall, cellulose,* and *chloroplast.* Students use these words in their responses to review questions on the unit during Inside/Outside Circle. For example, students are asked to describe what a cell wall is composed of. A student responds by saying, "A plant *cell wall* is composed of specialized sugars called *cellulose.*"

Strategies for the Classroom (cont.)

Parallel Lines

Overview

This strategy requires students to form two lines facing each other. At the teacher's signal, one line moves, while the other remains stationary. Each time a line moves, the teacher provides a question or prompt allowing students to exchange information. This strategy helps students orally practice using academic language within their responses.

Standards

- **McREL:** Students will use level-appropriate vocabulary in speech.

- **TESOL:** Students will use English to obtain, process, construct, and provide subject matter information in spoken and written form.

Directions

To incorporate this strategy, do the following:

1. Divide the class into two equal groups. Ask one group to line up in the front of the room. Instruct the other group to form another line facing the first group so that each student is facing a partner.

2. Give a prompt or question for students to discuss. After students have had a few moments to formulate a response, they share their answer with a partner.

3. After sharing, direct students to move one space to the left. Students at the end of each line move to the front of their line. Students should now have a new partner with whom to share or discuss.

Differentiating by Proficiency Level

Beginning:
Provide students with a set of prepared answers or statements they can share during this activity.

Intermediate:
Give students a list of questions you will be asking in the order they will be asked. Next to each question, provide a sentence frame (see page 120) for students to reference during the activity, if needed.

Advanced:
Give students a list of potential sentence starters or lists of words to use as a reference during the activity.

Strategies for the Classroom (cont.)

Parallel Lines (cont.)

Below are examples of how this strategy can be incorporated in a lesson.

Grades 1–2

Text Topic: Fossils

Example: The teacher divides students into two groups and has them form two lines facing each other. The teacher holds up pictures of fossils for students to look at. Beneath each picture is a sentence frame for students to use when responding to their partner. The teacher holds up a picture with the frame *This is a fossil of a _____. I think this because _____.* The teacher says, "I would like you to look at this picture and use this sentence to tell your partner what kind of fossil this might be." Students discuss with their partner and then move one spot to the left to face a new partner.

Grades 3–5

Text Topic: Planets

Example: The teacher divides students into two groups and has them form two lines facing each other. Students are given the following list of terms, which includes both specialized content and general academic vocabulary for the topic: *solar system*, *orbit*, *astronaut*, *travel*, *satellite*, *star*, and *astronomy*. Students use these words in their responses to review questions on the unit during Parallel Lines. For example, the teacher asks students to describe to their partner how the planets orbit the sun. The activity continues until all of the review questions have been asked.

Grades 6–8

Text Topic: Atoms

Example: The teacher divides students into two groups and has them form two lines facing each other. Students are given the following list of terms, which includes both specialized content and general academic vocabulary for the topic: *atoms*, *substance*, *protons*, *electrons*, *atomic number*, *element*, *periodic table*, and *symbol*. Students use these words in their responses to review questions on the unit during Parallel Lines. For example, the teacher asks students to describe to their partner how the periodic table is arranged. The activity continues until all of the review questions have been asked.

Strategies for the Classroom (cont.)

Clock Appointments

Overview

This strategy is an impromptu activity that allows students to set appointments and share answers to questions or prompts the teacher presents to them. Effective use of this strategy allows students the opportunity to use academic language with various classmates.

Standards

- **McREL:** Students will use level-appropriate vocabulary in speech.

- **TESOL:** Students will use English to obtain, process, construct, and provide subject matter information in spoken and written form.

Directions

To incorporate this strategy, do the following:

1. Prior to the lesson, make copies of page 165 for each student.

2. Distribute copies of the clock to students and explain that the numbers *12, 3, 6,* and *9* designate the four appointments students will have to set.

3. Allow students five minutes to mingle. While students mingle, they must make four appointments. Each appointment must be recorded on the clock next to the agreed-upon time. It is very important that each student making an appointment record it on his or her clock to avoid "double-booking."

4. Once each student has set all four appointments, ask them to return to their desks. At various points throughout the lesson or throughout the day, tell students to meet with one of their appointments to discuss a prompt or question.

Differentiating by Proficiency Level

Beginning:
Have students schedule the first two appointments with the teacher. During these appointments, practice the questions or prompts with students. Front-loading students with questions offers students the opportunity to practice the language.

Intermediate:
Give students the questions ahead of time and give them a few moments to jot down some of their thoughts for each question. When it is time for students to partner with peers, students will already have had some time to think about how they are going to respond.

Advanced:
Provide students with sentence frames (see page 120) appropriate to the prompts they will discuss in order to help them practice their use of academic language.

Strategies for the Classroom (cont.)

Clock Appointments (cont.)

Below are examples of how this strategy can be incorporated in a lesson.

Grades 1–2

Text Topic: Single-Digit Addition

Example: Students complete four addition problems on their own and meet with their appointments to see if they have the same answers. The teacher provides the following sentence frame as a guide: *I added the number _____ and the number _____. My sum was _____.* Students practice discussing their answers using this frame for each appointment.

Grades 3–5

Text Topic: New England Colonies

Example: During a lesson on the settlement of New England, the teacher asks students to set up Clock Appointments with classmates. Students are given the following list of both specialized content and general academic vocabulary to use during the discussions they have with their appointments: *settlers, resources, alliances, agriculture, Powhatan,* and *fur trade.* Students are told that they will discuss the following prompt with their first appointment: *Describe the relationship between the settlers and the Native Americans during this time.* As students watch a short video clip, they gather the information needed to answer this prompt. When the clip is over, students meet with their scheduled appointment.

Grades 6–8

Text Topic: Mathematical Reasoning

Example: As a warm-up, students are assigned four mathematical problems and given a set amount of time to work on the first problem. When they have finished, students meet with their first appointment to share their work. Students then return to work on the second problem before meeting with the next appointment. They continue until all of the problems have been solved and they have met with all of their scheduled appointments.

Strategies for the Classroom (cont.)

Fishbowl

Overview

This strategy allows students to observe a discussion after having had time to discuss it themselves. Once students have finished their discussions, the observers can ask clarifying questions. This strategy gives students the chance to practice using academic language while also providing the opportunity to be a "spectator" by listening to their peers use academic language without the pressure of participation.

Standards

- **McREL:** Students will use level-appropriate vocabulary in speech.

- **TESOL:** Students will use English to obtain, process, construct, and provide subject matter information in spoken and written form.

Directions

To incorporate this strategy, do the following:

1. Assign students to small groups for discussion.

2. Give each group a topic to discuss. Allow a few minutes for each group to brainstorm and determine how they will answer the discussion topic.

3. Direct one group to sit inside the "fishbowl" (in the middle of the other groups) while the other students are outside so they can observe the discussion. Allow the Fishbowl group to discuss its topic and tell the other students that they are to listen.

4. After the Fishbowl group finishes its discussion, the other students can comment or ask questions. The activity can be repeated with another group.

Differentiating by Proficiency Level

Beginning:
Provide students with sentence frames (see page 120) that model appropriate ways to start a comment or ask a question about what they have heard.

Intermediate:
Before the activity begins, give students the prompt they will be asked to discuss and allow them a few minutes to jot down some of their thoughts. Encourage students to use these notes during the discussion.

Advanced:
Encourage students to create their own questions or prompts to ask during their discussion time.

Strategies for the Classroom *(cont.)*

Fishbowl *(cont.)*

Below are examples of how this strategy can be incorporated in a lesson.

Grades 1–2

Text Topic: Story Elements

Example: Students in a Fishbowl group are provided with the following sentence frame: *The setting of the story was _____. I know this because _____.* Each student participates by holding up the sentence strip, completing the sentences out loud, then passing it to the next student in the Fishbowl, who would then generate his or her own response.

Grades 3–5

Text Topic: Persuasive Writing

Example: As a prewriting skill-building activity, students inside the Fishbowl are given a topic they will be debating. The following is the issue students are debating: *Everyone should have to finish all of their lunch before they go to recess.* Students inside the Fishbowl will debate the topic, discussing why they agree or disagree with the statement, while the rest of the class watches. After hearing students' responses, students write a persuasive essay on their topic.

Grades 6–8

Text Topic: Persuasive Writing/Speaking

Example: As a prewriting skill-building activity, students inside the Fishbowl are given a topic they will be debating. The following is the issue students are debating: *Children under 18 should not be allowed to buy or rent violent video games.* Students inside the Fishbowl will debate the topic, discussing why they agree or disagree with the statement, while the rest of the class listens. After hearing students' responses, students write a persuasive essay on their topic. Students will then read their essays to their classmates.

Strategies for the Classroom *(cont.)*

Passing the Pen

Overview

This strategy encourages thinking and writing skills as students work together in a team to answer a question or prompt presented to them. This strategy allows students the opportunity to use academic language with classmates.

Standards

- **McREL:** Students will use level-appropriate vocabulary in speech.

- **TESOL:** Students will use English to obtain, process, construct, and provide subject matter information in spoken and written form.

Directions

To incorporate this strategy, do the following:

1. Number students off into small groups of three or four. Provide each group with a pen and a sheet of paper (see page 166).

2. Assign a number to each student. Pose a question or prompt to students and call out a number. The student with the selected number will begin the activity at each table. Allow students to generate a brief response to the question or prompt. While students are responding to the question or prompt in each group, the other group members should remain silent.

3. At the teacher's signal, the pen is passed to the student with the next selected number, who adds to the response, agreeing, disagreeing, or elaborating on what has been written.

4. Students continue to pass the pen until everyone has had a turn.

Differentiating by Proficiency Level

Beginning:
Provide students a sheet with cloze sentences and a word bank for them to fill in rather than a blank sheet of paper. Have students read the short sentence and choose the word that fits best in the blank space before passing it to the next person in the group.

Intermediate:
Provide students with a free pass to use once during the activity if they are having trouble generating an original response.

Advanced:
Have students write a summary of their classmates' responses and ask them to write if they agree or disagree with their responses.

Strategies for the Classroom (cont.)

Passing the Pen (cont.)

Below are examples of how this strategy can be incorporated in a lesson.

Grades 1–2

Text Topic: Word Families

Example: The teacher arranges the class into small groups of four or five. Each group receives a sheet of paper with the base of the word family (rime) -*ack* repeated 10 times. The goal for each group is to create 10 words that belong to this word family (e.g., *tack, back, quack, smack, sack*). At the teacher's signal, the first student begins by adding a letter or letters (onset) to the beginning of the rime to form a word. Once they have written their word, they pass the pen and paper to the next person.

Grades 3–5

Text Topic: Compare and Contrast

Example: As a closing activity to a lesson on identifying words in text or writing that signals compare and contrast, the class is divided into small groups of four or five students. Each group has one sheet of paper and one pen. At the teacher's signal, students are prompted to generate a list of as many compare-and-contrast signal words as they can in a given amount of time (e.g., *instead, both, same, like*). Once a student has written down a word, the pen and paper is passed to the next student.

Grades 6–8

Text Topic: Plate Tectonics

Example: Students are grouped and given one sheet of paper and one pen per group. The teacher then calls off the list of words they will focus on in order to activate prior knowledge: *plate, stress, crust, focus,* and *fault*. At the teacher's signal, the first word, *plate* is called out. The teacher gives each group three minutes to write down either the different definitions of the word or a sentence using the word to show one of its meanings. When the first student writing a response has finished, the pen is passed to the next student. This student reads the response and writes a response showing a different meaning for the word *plate*. Each group continues to pass the pen until everyone has had a turn.

Strategies for the Classroom (cont.)

Gallery Walk

Overview

This strategy requires students to visually represent their knowledge to the unit of study. This strategy allows students to explore the usage of academic language in a low-stress environment while receiving feedback from their peers.

Standards

- **McREL:** Students will use level-appropriate vocabulary in speech.

- **TESOL:** Students will use English to obtain, process, construct, and provide subject matter information in spoken and written form.

Directions

To incorporate this strategy, do the following:

1. Place students into small groups of three or four and provide them with a question or prompt.

2. Tell students to work together to "show what they know" on their poster. Decide how they will represent their knowledge (e.g., graphic organizer, picture, outline).

3. When students have finished their posters, they post them around the room.

4. Tell students to travel as a group to visit the other posters in the room. The teacher can decide how feedback will be given. (e.g., Will students leave notes to the other groups? Will students revise their own poster when they are done?)

Differentiating by Proficiency Level

Beginning:	Intermediate:	Advanced:
Students can share their ideas, and classmates in their group can help generate the appropriate language on the group's poster.	Encourage students to discuss their answers with their group members.	Ask students to paraphrase what they have learned from the activity.

Strategies for the Classroom (cont.)

Gallery Walk (cont.)

Below are examples of how this strategy can be incorporated in a lesson.

Grades 1–2

Text Topic: Map Skills

Example: Students work together in small groups of three or four to create a poster-size map of the classroom. The teacher lists *flag*, *door*, *clock*, *shelves*, *tables*, and *bulletin boards* as items that must be a part of the map legend. Each group creates its own symbol for each of these items as they place them on the map. When each group is finished, the maps are hung and numbered. Students then travel in groups to visit each poster and discuss what they see. Students are given a sheet with questions to answer at each poster. For example, *Where is the legend located on map 4?*

Grades 3–5

Text Topic: Multiple-Step Word Problems

Example: Students are arranged into small groups and given a sheet of poster paper and a different multiple-step word problem to solve. For example, *In Ms. Mott's desk drawer, there are 18 black markers. There are 5 more pink markers than black markers, and there are 8 more green markers than pink markers. How many markers are there in all?* Each group must solve the word problem. They have the option to illustrate, write number sentences, or write sentences showing how they solved the problem. Each group then visits other posters and sees what strategies their classmates used.

Grades 6–8

Text Topic: Multiple-Step Word Problems

Example: Students are arranged into small groups and given a sheet of poster paper and a different multiple-step word problem to solve. For example, *A farmer grows 252 pounds of apples. He wants to sell some in 5-lb. bags and some in 2-lb. bags. If the farmer uses the same number of 5-lb. bags as 2-lb. bags, then how many bags will he use in all?* Each group must solve their word problem and show their work. They have the option to illustrate, write number sentences, or write sentences showing how they solved the problem. Each group travels together to visit each poster and discuss the work on the poster to determine if it is correct.

Resources

• • • • • • • • • • • •

Think-Write-Pair-Share Journal

Name _____

Directions: Listen to the question or prompt your teacher gives you. Write your response below. When you are finished, find a partner and talk about what each of you wrote. Write your partner's response below. Then listen to what your classmates share and write their responses below.

I think: _____

_____

_____

_____

We think: _____

_____

_____

_____

The class thinks: _____

_____

_____

_____

Resources (cont.)

Talking Chips

Resources *(cont.)*

● ● ● ● ● ● ● ● ● ● ● ● ● ● ● ●

Not Taboo

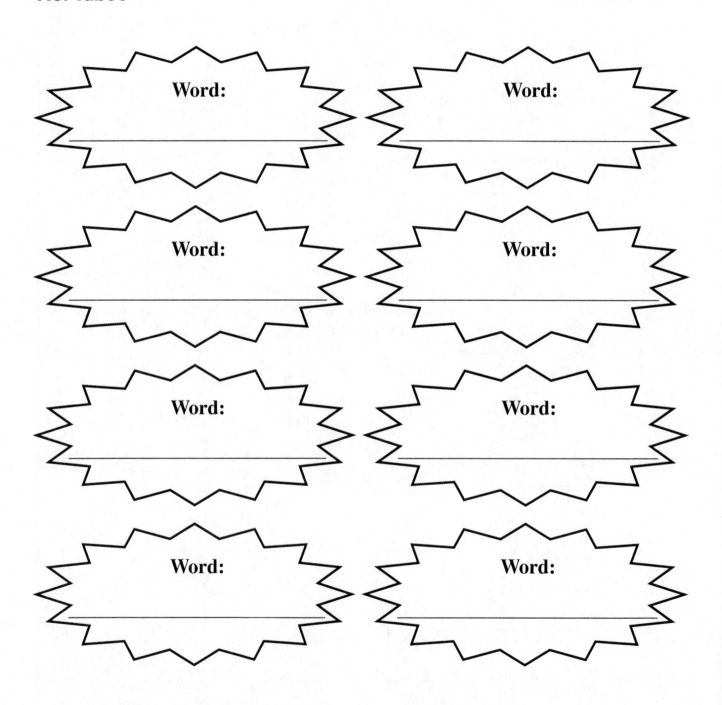

162

Resources

• • • • • • • • • • • •

Mix-Freeze-Match

Word: _____

_____

_____

_____

_____

_____

Word: _____

_____

_____

_____

_____

_____

Word: _____

_____

_____

_____

_____

_____

Resources (cont.)

● ● ● ● ● ● ● ● ● ● ● ● ● ● ● ●

Give and Take

Name _____

Directions: Listen to the question or prompt your teacher gives you. Write your answer below on the *Give* lines. Share your answer with a partner. Write any new ideas or information your partner shared with you on the *Take* lines. Listen to the whole-class discussion. Write any new ideas or information you hear in the *Our thoughts* lines.

Give: _____

_____

_____

_____

Take: _____

_____

_____

_____

Our thoughts: _____

_____

_____

_____

_____

_____

Resources (cont.)

Clock Appointments

Name _____

Directions: Find four classmates and put their names on the lines below. Listen to your teacher to find out when to meet with your appointments.

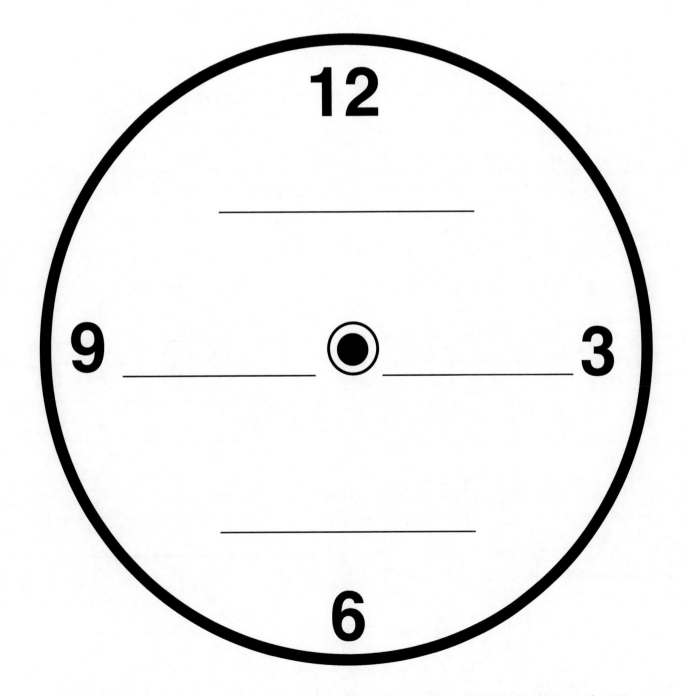

Resources *(cont.)*

· · · · · · · · · · · · · · ·

Passing the Pen

Names _____

Directions: Listen to the question or prompt your teacher gives you. At your teacher's signal, write your answer. When your teacher signals to pass the pen, pass this paper and pen to someone else in your group.

_____

_____

_____

_____

_____

_____

_____

_____

_____

_____

_____

_____

_____

_____

Lesson Design

What Makes a Good Lesson?

While there are many models and philosophies that define effective teaching, common elements exist among all models. Good teaching assumes the following:

- Lessons are carefully planned by the instructor, with consideration given to the needs of all students in the classroom.

- Lessons build on previous knowledge and prepare students for future learning.

- Teachers have meaningful and timely ways to measure student learning.

Regardless of the lesson design or planning template that is used, an effective lesson should contain the following components:

- **Clear Objective:** This should be stated and understood by students so a purpose for learning is established.

- **Opportunities for Student Response:** Responses can be interactions between the teacher and student or between students. Responses can be oral, written, or with the use of gestures, such as a thumbs-up or -down in response to a question or prompt.

- **Wait Time:** Ample wait time is particularly important for English language learners who are processing the content they are learning while also formulating the language they will use for their responses.

- **Monitored Student Responses:** This gives teachers an indication of how well students understand the material and allows them to adjust instruction during the lesson, if necessary.

- **Opportunities for Practice:** Providing time for practice during the lesson gives teachers the chance to monitor students and provide immediate feedback.

Elements of Lesson Design

A Horizontal Format

Typically, lesson-planning templates follow a vertical format in which the teacher fills in each section as he or she goes down the list. During lesson delivery, the tendency is also to follow the vertical format, moving down the list step by step. Sound familiar?

However, we are advocating a horizontal template with all of the same elements of a lesson but with a different delivery.

- **The body of the lesson should include several cycles of input, modeling, and checking for understanding.** By breaking the body of the lesson into cycles, the teacher can break the input into more comprehensible chunks for students. After teaching a point of input, the teacher can model briefly and check for understanding before moving to the next piece of input. The cycle then continues until all of the input has been given. (By constrast, the vertical lesson implies that all of the input is provided at once, then the teacher models all of the steps combined, and a quick check for understanding is done before students are moved to guided practice.)

- **The recursive cycle lesson allows teachers to determine which pieces of the lesson may need to be retaught or reviewed (concepts, skills, vocabulary, or language).** By contrast, waiting for all input and modeling to happen before checking for understanding makes it harder to determine whether students misunderstood the lesson as a whole or if perhaps they just need clarification on a point or two.

- Additionally, **breaking the lesson into cycles allows for scaffolding and provides ample opportunities for students to actively participate.** For example, when providing the check that will be the segue into the next piece of input, teachers can have students talk to one another, get up and move around the room, think about a question, or write on a response board. Students get a break in the learning to review and clarify, and perhaps even to speak.

- Often, if students know they are going to get this opportunity, they are more likely to pay attention. **Frequent checking for understanding provides a measure of student accountability.** Students know that the teacher is going to stop several times to monitor their learning, so they pay attention to be prepared.

To make checking for understanding work for both students and teachers, teachers should design checks that are not only frequent but also check the learning of all students, particularly English language learners.

Anticipatory Set:	Objective:	
Input:	Modeling:	Check for Understanding:
Guided Practice:		
Closure:		Independent Practice:

Elements of Lesson Design (cont.)

The sample lessons provided in this section (pages 176–190) are based on Madeline Hunter's model of direct instruction developed in the 1970s. Hunter suggested that there are eight elements that are generally (though not always) present in an effective lesson. The eight elements are present in the Horizontal Lesson Design Template and are listed on the table below and the next page as well. This table demonstrates how the preplanning that was done on the Academic Language Support Planning Template can be integrated into the Horizontal Lesson Design Template.

Horizontal Lesson Design Template	Academic Language Support Planning Template
Objective: This should specify what students will learn during the lesson and how they will demonstrate this learning. Teachers plan the objective based on curriculum standards and develop the rest of the lesson to meet that goal. The objective and purpose for learning should be shared with students in a student-friendly manner.	• Identify the *specialized content*, *general academic*, and *everyday* vocabulary students will need to comprehend. • Identify the linguistic *features* of the text. • Identify the *functions* of the language used in the text.
Anticipatory Set: Sometimes referred to as the "hook" of the lesson, this is a quick activity, question, or prompt at the start of the lesson that is intended to grab students' attention and allow students to tap into any prior knowledge that will be relevant to the new learning.	• Preview selected *specialized content* vocabulary. • Consider incorporating strategies that support *Schema and Vocabulary Building*, and/or *Comprehensible Input*.
Input: This should be all the information students will need to meet the lesson objective. It includes vocabulary, processes, facts, and other information. It can be presented orally, through reading, in a video, or with virtually any medium one uses to obtain information.	• Teach the linguistic *features* of the text. • Teach the *functions* of the language used in the text. • Consider incorporating strategies that support *Schema and Vocabulary Building*, and/or *Comprehensible Input*.
Modeling: The teacher demonstrates how students can use the new information. Sometimes teachers use a physical demonstration, a step-by-step explanation, or thinking aloud. This shows students how to apply their learning and models how they will be expected to demonstrate it.	• Use *specialized content*, *general academic*, and/or *everyday* vocabulary. • Teach the *functions of language* used in the text. • Consider incorporating strategies that support *Schema and Vocabulary Building*, *Comprehensible Input*, and/or *Opportunities for Practice*.

Elements of Lesson Design *(cont.)*

Horizontal Lesson Design Template	Academic Language Support Planning Template
Check for Understanding: Checking for student understanding is essential to ensure that students are ready to practice. If many students cannot demonstrate understanding, then the teacher should reteach before moving on. Pausing to check for understanding also allows students to verify that they are accurately following along.	• Include *specialized content*, *general academic*, and/or *everyday* vocabulary. • Teach the *functions* of the language used in the text. • Consider incorporating strategies that support *Schema and Vocabulary Building* and/or *Opportunities for Practice*.
Guided Practice: This happens when most students are ready to move on to work problems, conduct an experiment, or complete a task designed to allow them to practice what they have just learned. Students work independently or in groups. The teacher is available to answer questions, provide support, and give feedback.	• Include *specialized content*, *general academic*, and/or *everyday* vocabulary. • Teach the *functions* of the language used in the text. • Consider incorporating strategies that support *Schema and Vocabulary Building* and/or *Opportunities for Practice*.
Closure: Closure is a brief activity, prompt, or question that brings an end to the lesson. It helps students summarize and review what they have just learned and can help them cognitively "organize" the information. Students also get a chance to clarify and reinforce key points in the learning. Later, these key points will become essential to their ability to retrieve the information.	• Include *specialized content*, *general academic*, and/or *everyday* vocabulary. • Assess students' use of the *functions* of the language used in the text. • Consider incorporating strategies that support *Schema and Vocabulary Building* and/or *Opportunities for Practice*.
Independent Practice: At the conclusion of the lesson, independent practice allows for reinforcement and mastery. This means that students should really only be given independent practice once they have demonstrated mastery. It is important that the independent practice provides students the opportunity to use the information in different forms rather than in simply the approximate way it was taught.	• Include *specialized content*, *general academic*, and/or *everyday* vocabulary. • Practice the *functions* of the language used in the text. • Consider incorporating strategies that support *Schema and Vocabulary Building* and/or *Opportunities for Practice*.

Reviewing the Academic Language Support Planning Template *(cont.)*

Supporting the English Language Learner

In the previous four sections we explored the elements of lesson planning by using the horizontal template. Now we can focus on putting together content-area lessons using a template designed to support English language learners and academic language.

The Academic Language Support Planning Template

The template below will aid teachers in designing lessons when looking through the lens of academic language. In the next few pages, each quadrant will be reviewed. Furthermore, teachers will see this template being integrated within planning sample lessons.

The top half of the template (see below) addresses the questions posed in the Planning for Explicit Teaching section (pages 19–34). When planning, consider both the sources of information from which students will learn (e.g., text, video, computer) and the tasks they will be expected to complete. When completing the quadrants in this section, teachers should ask themselves the following questions:

- What is the specialized content vocabulary that might be unfamiliar to students?

- What general academic vocabulary might students need in order to comprehend the text and generate quality written and oral responses during the lesson?

- Is everyday vocabulary used in an unfamiliar way in the text (e.g., are there words with multiple meanings that need to be identified for students)?

- Are there other linguistic features of text specific to this genre that need to be identified for students (e.g., sentence structure, voice, grammatical features)?

- Which cognitive functions of language are used in the text (e.g., will students be expected to compare and contrast, recognize cause and effect, classify and categorize)?

Planning for Explicit Teaching			
Vocabulary			Language
Specialized Content:	General Academic:	Everyday:	Features: Functions:

Reviewing the Academic Language Support Planning Template *(cont.)*

The bottom half of the template addresses the strategies teachers will use for schema and vocabulary building, comprehensible input, and opportunities for practice.

The first box considers schema building and the need to present new content in a way in which all students can connect to prior knowledge. The teacher plans the lesson with each student's background and prior experiences in mind. Some of the questions the teacher might want to think about while planning this piece include the following:

- What are my students' levels of experience with this new content? How will I assess this?

- Is the format of the text new to my students (e.g., have they been presented with history using historical narrative before)?

- If I have found that my students need to create schema on the new topic, how will I do this (e.g., video, realia, books on the topic)?

The next box is for planning how to make input comprehensible for students during the lesson. Going back to the section on Comprehensible Input (pages 107–132), some of the ways teachers can do this include the following:

- delivering lessons using multiple modalities

- scaffolding

- using study guides

- providing sentence frames

- using graphic organizers

Strategies		
Schema and Vocabulary Building:	Comprehensible Input:	Opportunities for Practice:

Reviewing the Academic Language Support Planning Template *(cont.)*

The last planning consideration concerns opportunities for practice. To make the most of giving students the opportunity to discuss and use the content they are learning, the teacher should make sure that the activities are well planned. This might include choosing the active participation structures in advance and having any necessary materials (papers, chips/tokens, sticky notes, timers) readily available. Planning the questions or prompts students will write about and/or discuss can also go a long way in delivering an effective lesson. Some considerations include the following:

- What active participation strategies will I use? Are students aware of how to use these strategies?

- What questions will I ask students to discuss or write about?

- What support might students need in order to be successful in practice (e.g., sentence frames, lists of target vocabulary)?

Reviewing the Academic Language Support Planning Template *(cont.)*

Planning Template Quick Reference

For further support, refer to this quick reference template to remind you of the essential components of each quadrant while planning through the lens of academic language.

Planning for Explicit Teaching			
Vocabulary			**Language**
Specialized Content: Is there specialized vocabulary that might be unfamiliar to students? (e.g., *stamen, pistil*)	General Academic: What general academic vocabulary might students need to comprehend the text and generate quality written and oral responses during the lesson? (e.g., *analyze, explain*)	Everyday: Are there everyday words in the passage that are used in an unfamiliar way? (e.g., *table*)	Features: Are there linguistic features of text specific to this genre that need to be identified for students (e.g., sentence structure, voice, grammatical features)? Functions: What cognitive functions of the language are used in the text (e.g., will students be expected to compare and contrast, recognize cause and effect)?
Strategies			
Schema and Vocabulary Building: • What are my students' levels of experience with this new content? How will I assess this? • Is the format of the text new to my students (e.g., have they been presented with history using historical narrative before)? • If I have found that my students need to create schema on the new topic, how will I do this (e.g., video, realia, books on the topic)?	Comprehensible Input: Delivering lessons using multiple modalities such as the following: • scaffolding • providing time for guided practice • using study guides • providing sentence frames • using graphic organizers	Opportunities for Practice: • What active participation strategies will I use? Are students aware of how to use these strategies? • What are some of the questions I will ask students to discuss or write about? • What support might students need to be successful in practice (e.g., sentence frames, lists of target vocabulary)?	

Sample Lessons

Point of View Lesson

Consider how the individual elements of the planning template come together when planning a language arts lesson on point of view. Take a look at both sample texts below. The text on the left is part of the familiar story of *The Story of the Three Little Pigs* (Brooke 1904). The text on the right is part of *The True Story of the Three* *Little Pigs* (Scieszka and Smith 1996) told from the wolf's point of view. As you read the text, think about how the lesson design template can be completed in preparation for building academic language during this language arts lesson.

The Story of the Three Little Pigs
(excerpt from *The Story of the Three Little Pigs*)

The first that went off met a Man with a bundle of straw, and said to him, "Please, Man, give me that straw to build me a house"; which the Man did, and the little Pig built a house with it. Presently came along a Wolf, and knocked at the door, and said, "Little Pig, little Pig, let me come in."

To which the Pig answered, "No, no, by the hair of my chinny chin chin."

"Then I'll huff and I'll puff, and I'll blow your house in!" said the Wolf. So he huffed and he puffed, and he blew his house in, and ate up the little Pig.

The True Story of the Three Little Pigs
(excerpt from *The True Story of the Three Little Pigs*)

Everybody knows the story of the Three Little Pigs. Or at least they think they do. But I'll let you in on a little secret. Nobody knows the real story, because nobody has ever heard my side of the story… But like I was saying, the whole big bad wolf thing is all wrong. The real story is about a sneeze and a cup of sugar.

Sample Lessons *(cont.)*

Point of View Lesson *(cont.)*

Here is an example of a completed lesson design template for this lesson on point of view.

Planning for Explicit Teaching			
Vocabulary			**Language**
Specialized Content: • first person • third person • point of view	General Academic: • compare • contrast	Everyday: • hear • see	Features: • author writing in first person and third person Functions: • compare/contrast
Strategies			
Schema and Vocabulary Building: • Quick-Write • Word-Definition Map	Comprehensible Input: • Study Guides • Sentence Frames: ▸ In both stories _____, but in _____. ▸ In one story _____ happened, but in the other story _____.		Opportunities for Practice: • Think-Pair-Share • Think-Write-Pair-Share • Talking Chips

Sample Lessons (cont.)

Point of View Lesson (cont.)

Let's take the completed lesson design template (page 177) and integrate a grid that demonstrates how a recursive cycle can be designed by a teacher to break up the input and provide multiple input/modeling/check for understanding cycles. Each step is explained on pages 179–180.

Anticipatory Set:	Objective:	
Ask students to retell *The Story of the Three Little Pigs* using the **Study Guides** strategy. Write the key elements of the story on a sheet of chart paper. Review the major events from the story and explain that from this version of the story it is clear that the wolf is the instigator and the three pigs are portrayed as the victims.	Students will analyze differences in literary works in terms of point of view by **comparing and contrasting** *The Story of the Three Little Pigs* and *The True Story of the Three Little Pigs*.	

Input:	Modeling:	Check for Understanding:
1. Introduce students to **Vocabulary**. Use a **Word-Defintion Map** for the vocabulary word *point of view*.	1. Read the sample text. Point out the key words that indicate the point of view.	1. **Think-Pair-Share:** How does point of view affect how a story is told?
2. Read sample text of *The True Story of the Three Little Pigs* aloud to the class.	2. Select two points to stop and discuss what may be different from the original version. Explain that the wolf is telling the story in first person.	2. **Think-Pair-Share:** How might the events be told differently if one of the pigs were telling the story?
3. Describe an event that was told differently in each story using **Sentence Frames** for comparing and contrasting.	3. Use **Sentence Frames** while discussing the events.	3. **Think-Pair-Share:** How did point of view influence how the events were told?

Guided Practice:	
Have students work in small groups integrating the **Talking Chips** strategy to **compare and contrast** events explaining how they think the point of view may have changed how the event was told.	

Closure:	Independent Practice:
Ask students, "How can point of view influence how a story is told?" Have students do a **Think-Write-Pair-Share**.	Ask students to think about a time they shared their point of view with someone. Have students do a **Quick-Write** explaining this.

Sample Lessons (cont.)

Point of View Lesson (cont.)

Anticipatory Set: The teacher asks students to retell *The Story of the Three Little Pigs*. As they engage in a class discussion, the teacher uses the **Study Guides** strategy and writes down key elements of the story on a sheet of chart paper. When the discussion has finished, the teacher reviews the major events from the story and explains that from this version of the story, it is clear that the wolf is the instigator and the three pigs are portrayed as the victims.

Objective: Students will analyze differences in literary works in terms of point of view by comparing and contrasting *The Story of the Three Little Pigs* and *The True Story of the Three Little Pigs*. The teacher shares the objective with students in a student-friendly manner.

Input/Model/Check for Understanding Cycle 1

Input 1: The teacher shares with students that they will be reading a new story told from the point of view of the wolf. The teacher proceeds to do a **Word-Definition Map** to strengthen students' understanding of what *point of view* means. The term *point of view* is defined and explained to students as the way the author lets students (the readers) "hear" or "see" the story. The teacher proceeds to tell students that authors do this in three ways: *first-person*, *second-person*, and *third-person*. Students are told that for this particular lesson, they will be focusing on *first-person* and *third-person* versions of the stories. The original story, *The Story of the Three Little Pigs,* is told in third person because it sounds like an outsider is telling the story as he or she is watching it. It is the voice of an outsider and not of a character involved in the story. *The True Story of the Three Little Pigs* is told in first person because one of the characters is telling the story.

Model 1: The teacher reads the sample text from each story and is explicit in pointing out the key words that indicate the point of view from which the story is being told. The teacher also reminds students that *The Story of the Three Little Pigs* is written in third person, while *The True Story of the Three Little Pigs* is written in first person.

Check 1: The teacher asks students, "How does point of view affect how a story is told?" Students then work with a partner and do a **Think-Pair-Share** for this question. The teacher selects student volunteers to share their thoughts with the class.

Input/Model/Check for Understanding Cycle 2

Input 2: After students are finished discussing their thoughts on point of view, the teacher reads the sample text of *The True Story of the Three Little Pigs* aloud to the class.

Model 2: As the teacher reads the sample text, two main points have been selected where the teacher will stop and discuss how what has just happened in the story may be different from the original story. The teacher explains that because the wolf tells this story in first person, his point of view influences how he feels the event happened. Point of view can change how a story is told because everyone *sees* events differently. How we see or *hear* events is influenced by our involvement in the event, our past experiences, our feelings, opinions, and many other factors.

Check 2: Each time the teacher stops at a main point, the students are asked, "How did point of view influence how the events were told?" Students are asked to **Think-Pair-Share** with their partners.

Sample Lessons (cont.)

● ●

Point of View Lesson (cont.)

Input/Model/Check for Understanding Cycle 3

Input 3: The teacher selects an event that is told differently in each story and uses **Sentence Frames** with comparing and contrasting signal words and explains that the event was explained differently in each story based on who was doing the explaining.

Model 3: While discussing the event with students, the teacher uses **Sentence Frames** as a reference:

• In both stories _____, but in _____.

• In one story _____ happened, but in the other story _____.

The teacher uses these sentence frames to explain the similarities and differences between the two stories and events.

Check 3: The teacher refers to the event that was just explained, discussed, and modeled for students and asks students how they think point of view influenced how the event was told. Students are asked to do a Think-Pair-Share with a partner before sharing with the class.

Guided Practice: The teacher asks students to work in small groups while integrating the **Talking Chips** strategy to compare and contrast the events and explain how they think the point of view may have changed how the events were told.

Closure: The teacher leads a class discussion by asking students to explain how point of view can influence how a story is told. The teacher writes students' responses on a sheet of chart paper and asks students to complete a **Think-Write-Pair-Share** with the information that was reviewed and discussed.

Independent Practice: Students are asked to think about a time they shared their point of view with someone. After a few minutes, students do a **Quick-Write** explaining their experiences.

Sample Lessons (cont.)

Properties of Multiplication with Fractions Lesson

Consider how the individual elements of the planning template come together when planning a math lesson on the properties of multiplication with fractions. Take a look at the sample text below. As you read the text, think about how the lesson design template can be completed in preparation for building academic language during this mathematics lesson.

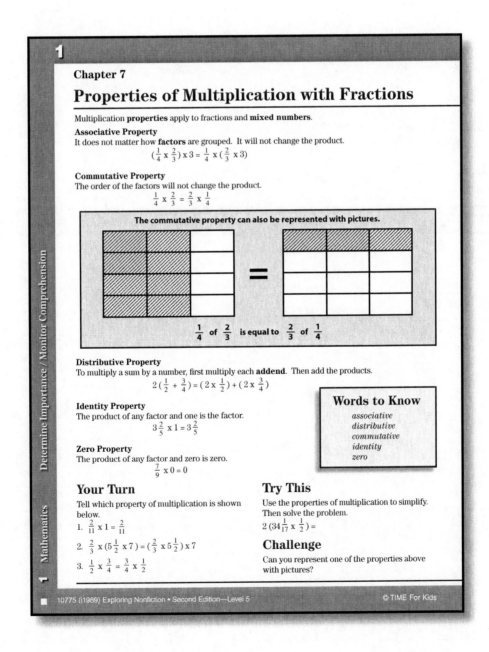

Chapter 7

Properties of Multiplication with Fractions

Multiplication **properties** apply to fractions and **mixed numbers**.

Associative Property
It does not matter how **factors** are grouped. It will not change the product.
$$(\tfrac{1}{4} \times \tfrac{2}{3}) \times 3 = \tfrac{1}{4} \times (\tfrac{2}{3} \times 3)$$

Commutative Property
The order of the factors will not change the product.
$$\tfrac{1}{4} \times \tfrac{2}{3} = \tfrac{2}{3} \times \tfrac{1}{4}$$

The commutative property can also be represented with pictures.

$$\tfrac{1}{4} \text{ of } \tfrac{2}{3} \text{ is equal to } \tfrac{2}{3} \text{ of } \tfrac{1}{4}$$

Distributive Property
To multiply a sum by a number, first multiply each **addend**. Then add the products.
$$2(\tfrac{1}{2} + \tfrac{3}{4}) = (2 \times \tfrac{1}{2}) + (2 \times \tfrac{3}{4})$$

Identity Property
The product of any factor and one is the factor.
$$3\tfrac{2}{5} \times 1 = 3\tfrac{2}{5}$$

Zero Property
The product of any factor and zero is zero.
$$\tfrac{7}{9} \times 0 = 0$$

Words to Know
associative
distributive
commutative
identity
zero

Your Turn

Tell which property of multiplication is shown below.
1. $\tfrac{2}{11} \times 1 = \tfrac{2}{11}$
2. $\tfrac{2}{3} \times (5\tfrac{1}{2} \times 7) = (\tfrac{2}{3} \times 5\tfrac{1}{2}) \times 7$
3. $\tfrac{1}{2} \times \tfrac{3}{4} = \tfrac{3}{4} \times \tfrac{1}{2}$

Try This

Use the properties of multiplication to simplify. Then solve the problem.
$2(34\tfrac{1}{17} \times \tfrac{1}{2}) =$

Challenge

Can you represent one of the properties above with pictures?

Determine Importance / Monitor Comprehension

Mathematics

10775 (i1989) Exploring Nonfiction • Second Edition—Level 5   © TIME For Kids

Sample Lessons *(cont.)*

Properties of Multiplication with Fractions Lesson *(cont.)*

Here is an example of a completed lesson design template for this lesson on multiplication with the fractions content-area text on the previous page.

Planning for Explicit Teaching			
Vocabulary			**Language**
Specialized Content:	General Academic:	Everyday:	Features:
• associative property • distributive property • commutative property • identity property • zero property	none	• is = equals • and = multiply • property	• text box showing example of numbers and words being used in a sentence $\frac{1}{4}$ of $\frac{2}{3}$ is equal to $\frac{2}{3}$ of $\frac{1}{4}$ Functions: • classify/categorize

Strategies		
Schema and Vocabulary Building:	Comprehensible Input:	Opportunities for Practice:
• Is It Possible? • Semantic Map:	• Visual Modality	• Pass the Pen • Think-Pair-Share • Think-Write-Pair-Share • Whip-Around • Give and Take

Semantic Map:

<u>Associative</u> (grouping does not matter)

<u>Commutative</u> (order does not matter)

Properties of Multiplication

<u>Zero</u> (the product of any factor and 0 is 0)

<u>Distributive</u> (first multiply each addend and then add the products)

<u>Identity</u> (the product of any factor and 1 is the factor)

Sample Lessons (cont.)

Properties of Multiplication with Fractions Lessons (cont.)

Once again, let us take the completed lesson design template from the properties of multiplication with fractions lesson (page 182) and integrate a grid that demonstrates how a recursive cycle can be designed to break up the input and provide multiple input/modeling/check for understanding cycles. Each step is explained on pages 184–185.

Anticipatory Set: Preview the five properties of multiplication. Ask students to explain one of them to a partner using **Pass the Pen**. Have students share what they discussed while responses are recorded on a chart-size **Semantic Map**.	Objective: Students will describe the five properties of multiplication by **classifying and categorizing** the different characteristics of each property.	
Input:	**Modeling:**	**Check for Understanding:**
1. Read about the commutative property.	1. Explain the property and show the illustration. Support the **Visual Modality** with an illustration.	1. Students explain the commutative property. Students copy the illustration onto their notes.
2. Read about the associative property.	2. Model the associative property using think-aloud.	2. **Think-Write-Pair-Share:** Students illustrate the property and check with a partner.
3. Read about the distributive property.	3. Model the distributive property using think-aloud.	3. **Think-Write-Pair-Share:** Students illustrate the distributive property and check with a partner.
4. Read about the identity and zero properties and highlight the words *is* and *and* in each description.	4. Explain how the terms *is* and *and* are used in mathematics, comparing the relationship between the words and numerical expressions.	4. **Think-Pair-Share:** Students complete the illustrations for the last two properties and compare their drawings with a partner.
5. Use completed illustrations as a **Visual Modality** to identify which property each problem is demonstrating.	5. Point to the first problem on the sample text and review each of the properties.	5. **Think-Pair-Share:** Students explain why the first equation demonstrates the identity property.
Guided Practice: Ask students to identify characteristics in the various properties by using **Give and Take**.		
Closure: Integrate the **Whip-Around** strategy and ask students to explain one of the properties of multiplication.	**Independent Practice:** Integrate the **Is It Possible?** strategy by giving students example and nonexample sentences using the vocabulary in practice.	

Sample Lessons (cont.)

Properties of Multiplication with Fractions Lesson (cont.)

Anticipatory Set: The teacher begins the lesson by previewing the five properties of multiplication. Students are asked to write down the properties they remember and to share with a partner using the **Pass the Pen** strategy. After a few minutes, the class shares their findings as the teacher records students' responses on a chart-size **Semantic Map**.

Objective: The teacher tells students that they will describe the five properties of multiplication. The teacher shares the objective with students in a student-friendly manner.

Input/Model/Check for Understanding Cycle 1

Input 1: Students are directed to the sample text and asked to read about the commutative property.

Model 1: The teacher models and explains the commutative property and directs students' attention to the illustration on the page, explaining the purpose of the illustration. Students examine the illustration to support the **Visual Modality**.

Check 1: Students explain the commutative property to partners. They then share their explanations and copy the illustration for the commutative property onto their notes.

Input/Model/Check for Understanding Cycle 2

Input 2: Once students are able to correctly explain the commutative property, the teacher moves on to the next step of input. Students continue by reading about the associative property within the text.

Model 2: The teacher models and explains the property, using think-aloud to demonstrate how to understand what the text is describing as associative property.

Check 2: Students complete a quick **Think-Write-Pair-Share**. Students illustrate the associative property and check it against a partner's illustration.

Input/Model/Check for Understanding Cycle 3

Input 3: Once students are able to correctly explain the associative property, the teacher moves on to the next step of input and essentially repeats this input-model-check cycle for the distributive property. Students continue by reading about the distributive property in the sample text.

Model 3: The teacher models and explains the property using a think-aloud to demonstrate how to understand what the text is describing as distributive property.

Check 3: Students complete a quick **Think-Write-Pair-Share**. Students illustrate the distributive property and check it against a partner's illustration.

Sample Lessons *(cont.)*

Properties of Multiplication with Fractions Lesson *(cont.)*

Input/Model/Check for Understanding Cycle 4

Input 4: The teacher reads identity and zero properties aloud, emphasizing the words *and* and *is* in each description.

Model 4: The teacher points to the highlighted words, "The product of any factor *and* one *is* the factor," and explains what those terms mean in mathematics, highlighting the relationship between the words and the numerical expressions.

Check 4: Students complete a **Think-Pair-Share**, and in their own words, explain the identity and zero properties. Afterwards, students complete the illustrations for the last two properties and compare their drawings with partners to check for accuracy. Once students are successful, the teacher does a second check for understanding relating the vocabulary that was just explained by integrating another **Think-Pair-Share**. The teacher asks students, "What do *is* and *and* mean in those definitions?"

Input/Model/Check for Understanding Cycle 5

Input 5: Students are directed to use their illustrations as a **Visual Modality** to identify which property is being demonstrated at the bottom of the sample text.

Model 5: The teacher points to the first problem on the sample text and does a think-aloud through each of the properties to model how to identify the correct property.

Check 5: Students complete a **Think-Pair-Share** by explaining to partners why the first equation demonstrates the identity property.

Guided Practice: Students are asked to identify which property is represented by the next two equations while integrating the **Give and Take** strategy.

Closure: The teacher asks students to close their notebooks and does a quick **Whip-Around**, asking students to explain one of the properties of multiplication from memory. Students may repeat a property that was already shared.

Independent Practice: The teacher uses the **Is It Possible?** strategy by giving students example and nonexample sentences using the vocabulary in practice.

Sample Lessons (cont.)

Protozoa Lesson

Consider how the individual elements of the planning template come together when planning a science lesson on protozoa. Take a look at the sample text below. As you read the text, think about how the lesson design template can be completed in preparation for building academic language during this science lesson.

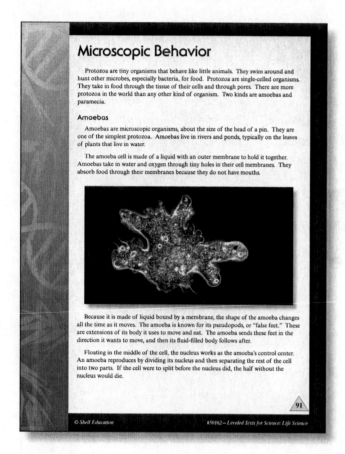

Microscopic Behavior

Protozoa are tiny organisms that behave like little animals. They swim around and hunt other microbes, especially bacteria, for food. Protozoa are single-celled organisms. They take in food through the tissue of their cells and through pores. There are more protozoa in the world than any other kind of organism. Two kinds are amoebas and paramecia.

Amoebas

Amoebas are microscopic organisms, about the size of the head of a pin. They are one of the simplest protozoa. Amoebas live in rivers and ponds, typically on the leaves of plants that live in water.

The amoeba cell is made of a liquid with an outer membrane to hold it together. Amoebas take in water and oxygen through tiny holes in their cell membranes. They absorb food through their membranes because they do not have mouths.

Because it is made of liquid bound by a membrane, the shape of the amoeba changes all the time as it moves. The amoeba is known for its pseudopods, or "false feet." These are extensions of its body it uses to move and eat. The amoeba sends these feet in the direction it wants to move, and then its fluid-filled body follows after.

Floating in the middle of the cell, the nucleus works as the amoeba's control center. An amoeba reproduces by dividing its nucleus and then separating the rest of the cell into two parts. If the cell were to split before the nucleus did, the half without the nucleus would die.

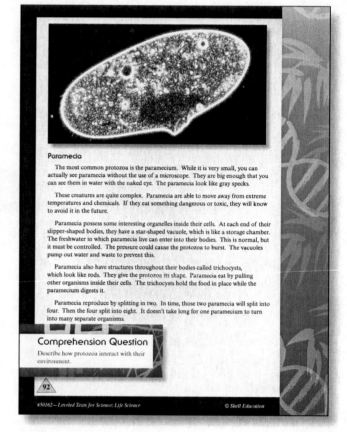

Paramecia

The most common protozoa is the paramecium. While it is very small, you can actually see paramecia without the use of a microscope. They are big enough that you can see them in water with the naked eye. The paramecia look like gray specks.

These creatures are quite complex. Paramecia are able to move away from extreme temperatures and chemicals. If they eat something dangerous or toxic, they will know to avoid it in the future.

Paramecia possess some interesting organelles inside their cells. At each end of their slipper-shaped bodies, they have a star-shaped vacuole, which is like a storage chamber. The freshwater in which paramecia live can enter into their bodies. This is normal, but it must be controlled. The pressure could cause the protozoa to burst. The vacuoles pump out water and waste to prevent this.

Paramecia also have structures throughout their bodies called trichocysts, which look like rods. They give the protozoa its shape. Paramecia eat by pulling other organisms inside their cells. The trichocysts hold the food in place while the paramecium digests it.

Paramecia reproduce by splitting in two. In time, those two paramecia will split into four. Then the four split into eight. It doesn't take long for one paramecium to turn into many separate organisms.

Comprehension Question

Describe how protozoa interact with their environment.

Sample Lessons (cont.)

Protozoa Lesson (cont.)

Here is an example of a completed lesson design template for this lesson on protozoa.

Planning for Explicit Teaching			
Vocabulary			**Language**
Specialized Content: • amoeba • protozoa • organism • membrane	General Academic: • reproduce	Everyday: • tissue	Features: • sentence structure Functions: • compare/contrast
Strategies			
Schema and Vocabulary Building: • Semantic Map: organism protozoa amoeba paramecium	Comprehensible Input: • Visual Modality • Study Guides (Venn diagram) • Sentence Frames: ▸ Amoebas split _____, but Paramecia split _____. ▸ Amoebas eat by _____, but Paramecia eat by _____.		Opportunities for Practice: • Think-Pair-Share • Think-Write-Pair-Share • In their own words, students can explain how an amoeba reproduces. ▸ Choose one of the paramecia's organelles. Explain what it is and how it works.

Sample Lessons *(cont.)*

Protozoa Lesson *(cont.)*

Now let us take the completed lesson design template from the protozoa lesson (page 187) and integrate a grid that demonstrates how a recursive cycle can be designed by a teacher to break up the input and provide multiple input/modeling/check for understanding cycles. Each step is explained on pages 189–190.

Anticipatory Set: Ask, "What creatures can you see under a microscope?" Support the **Visual Modality** by showing a picture.	Objective: Students will **compare/contrast** characteristics of different types of protozoa.	
Input: 1. Introduce students to vocabulary. 2. Read the sample text. 3. Ask students to read independently, highlighting key points. 4. Introduce **Sentence Frames** for **compare/contrast**.	**Modeling:** 1. Create a **Semantic Map** for the word *organism*. 2. Stop after each paragraph to add to the **Semantic Map**. Explain the meaning of the word *reproduce* in the last paragraph. 3. Review text with students. Stop again at the word *reproduce*. 4. Model using **Sentence Frames** to compare and contrast.	**Check for Understanding:** 1. **Think-Pair-Share:** Explain the relationship between the vocabulary words. 2. **Think-Pair-Share:** How do amoeba reproduce? 3. **Think-Write-Pair-Share:** Choose one of the paramecia's organelles. Explain what it is and how it works. 4. Have students write two **compare/contrast** statements using given **Sentence Frames**.
Guided Practice: Ask students to use the text, diagrams in their notebooks, and **Sentence Frames** to complete a Venn diagram (**Study Guides**) comparing the characteristics of the amoeba and paramecium.		
Closure: Using the **Think-Pair-Share** strategy, ask students to describe one important difference between the two organisms.	**Independent Practice:** Using notes, text, and **Sentence Frames**, have students write five statements **comparing and contrasting** amoebas and paramecia.	

Sample Lessons *(cont.)*

Protozoa Lesson *(cont.)*

Anticipatory Set: The teacher begins by showing students a microscope (or picture of a microscope) to support the **Visual Modality**. If students are not familiar with how it works, the teacher explains how a specimen is placed on the slide and looked at through the lens, which magnifies the very small particles that are on the slide so that they can be seen. Students are asked, "What creatures can you see under a microscope?" After allowing a moment for students to think, they share their thoughts with partners and then with the class.

Objective: Students will learn about tiny organisms called *protozoa*. They will **compare/contrast** the characteristics of two different types of protozoa. The teacher shares the objective with students in a student-friendly manner.

Input/Model/Check for Understanding Cycle 1

Input 1: The specialized content vocabulary words *amoeba, protozoa, organism*, and *membrane* are written on the board. Each word is explained, such as, "an *organism* is a living thing that has different parts, like organs, that work together to keep it alive. Humans are organisms, and so are plants, trees, and small things like germs. *Protozoa* are very tiny organisms that only have one cell but still have different parts in that cell. A *membrane* is a thin, pliable piece of animal or plant tissue (discuss the difference between how tissue is used here) that surrounds an organ. An *amoeba* are microscopic organisms that live in rivers and ponds."

Model 1: The relationship between the vocabulary words are modeled and explained using a **Semantic Map**.

Check 1: Students then explain the **Semantic Map** to partners using the **Think-Pair-Share** strategy. For example, "*Protozoa* is a type of *organism*. *Amoebas* and *paramecia* are types of *protozoa*."

Input/Model/Check for Understanding Cycle 2

Input 2: The sample text is read. Alternating reading is done between the teacher and students.

Model 2: The teacher models for students how to pause after each paragraph and describes something they should add to their **Semantic Maps**. For example, in the sample text the word *reproduce* appears in the last paragraph. The word is explained as it refers to science (e.g., producing or making another of the same kind). The teacher then tells students, "When an amoeba *reproduces*, it makes another amoeba. Protozoa can *reproduce* independently by splitting apart."

Check 2: After listening to the explanation and reading the last paragraph of the sample text, students now explain how an amoeba reproduces by using the **Think-Pair-Share** activity.

Sample Lessons (cont.)

Protozoa Lesson (cont.)

Input/Model/Check for Understanding Cycle 3

Input 3: Students read the text independently, highlighting any important information they will need in labeling their diagrams.

Model 3: The text is reviewed again. This time, the teacher stops and discusses the idea of reproduction again, pointing out how *reproduce* is used in the passage.

Check 3: Students use a practice strategy, such as **Think-Pair-Write-Share**, to explain how one of the organelles functions.

Input/Model/Check for Understanding Cycle 4

Input 4: Students use **Sentence Frames** as guides when discussing with their partners and/ or writing about what they have read. The following **Sentence Frames** are posted on the board to support the language that is needed to express comparisons:

• Amoebas split _____, but Paramecia split _____.

• Amoebas eat by _____, but Paramecia eat by _____.

Model 4: Students see and hear several examples of the correct use of the language in the frames.

Check 4: Students write two **compare/contrast** statements in their notebooks, based on the reading and the **Sentence Frames** they are given. When students have finished, students share their comparison statements.

Guided Practice: Students work on completing a Venn diagram as a **Study Guide** to compare and contrast the amoeba and paramecium. Students are encouraged to use the information they have written down as well as the comparisons they heard their classmates use during discussion.

Closure: Students are asked to describe one important difference between the amoeba and the paramecium. After students have time to generate a response, they do the **Think-Pair-Share** activity with partners.

Independent Practice: Students review their notes, text, and **Sentence Frames**. For homework, they write five compare and contrast statements about the amoeba and paramecium.

Resources

●●●●●●●●●●●

Horizontal Lesson Design Template

Anticipatory Set:	Objective:	
Input:	**Modeling:**	**Check for Understanding:**
Guided Practice:		
Closure:	**Independent Practice:**	

192

Additional Resources

References Cited

● ● ● ● ● ● ● ● ● ● ● ● ● ● ● ● ● ● ● ●

Anderson, R. C. 1984. Some reflections on the acquisition of knowledge. *Educational Researcher* 13(9): 5–10.

Bailey, A. and F.A. Butler. 2007. *The language demands of school: Putting academic English to the test.* Yale University Press.

Bailey, A. and M. Heritage. 2008. *Formative assessment for literacy grades K–6: Building reading and academic language skills across the curriculum.* Thousand Oaks, CA: Corwin Press.

Beck, I. L., M. G. McKeown, and E. W. Gromoll. 1989. Learning from social studies texts. *Cognition and Instruction* 6: 99–158.

Beck, I. L., M.G. McKeown, and L. Kucan. 2002. *Bringing words to life: Robust vocabulary instruction.* New York, NY: Guilford Press.

Blachowitz, C. and P. J. Fisher. 2002. *Teaching vocabulary in all classrooms*, 2nd ed. Upper Saddle River, NJ: Merrill Prentice Hall.

Carrell, P. L. and J. C. Eisterhold. 1983. Schema theory and ESL reading pedagogy. *TESOL Quarterly* 17 (4).

Carroll, Lewis. *Through the Looking-Glass.* United Kingdom: Macmillan, 1871.

Chamot, A. U. and J. M. O'Malley. 1996. The cognitive academic language learning approach (CALLA): A model for linguistically diverse classrooms. *Elementary School Journal* 96 (3): 259–73.

Colombi, M. C., and M.J. Schleppegrell 2002. In *Developing advanced literacy in first and second languages: Meaning with power*, eds. M. J. Schleppegrell and M. C. Colombi, 1-20. London: Lawrence Erlbaum Associates.

Coxhead, A. 2000. A new academic word list. *TESOL Quarterly* 34: 213–238.

Cummins, J. (2003). BICS and CALP: Origins and rationale for the distinction. In *Sociolinguistics: The essential readings*, eds. C. B. Paulston and G. R. Tucker, 322–28. Malden, MA: Blackwell.

Cuevas, G. J. 1984. Mathematics learning in English as a second language. *Journal of Research in Mathematics Education* 15 (2): 134–44.

de Jong, E. J. and C. A. Harper. 2005. Preparing mainstream teachers for English-language learners: Is being a good teacher good enough? *Teacher Education Quarterly* 32 (2): 101–24.

Droop, M. and L. T. Verhoeven. 1998. Background knowledge, linguistic complexity, and second language reading comprehension. *Journal of Literacy Research* 30 (2): 253–71.

Echevarria, J., D. Short, and K. Powers. 2006. School reform and standards-based education: A model for English language learners. *The Journal of Educational Research* 99 (4): 195–210.

Gibbons, P. 1998. *Learning to learn in a second language.* Portsmouth, NH: Heinemann.

Herrell, A., and M. Jordan. 2004. *Fifty strategies for teaching English language learners*. 2nd ed. Upper Saddle, NJ: Pearson Education, Inc.

References Cited (cont.)

Hofstadter, D. R. 1980. Translations of "Jabberwocky." Jabberwocky Variations. Retrieved from http://www76.pair.com/keithlim/jabberwocky/poem/hofstadter.html.

Hunter, M.1982. *Mastery teaching: Increasing instructional effectiveness in elementary, secondary schools, colleges and universities.* Thousand Oaks, CA: Corwin Press, Inc.

Johnson, R. T. and D. W. Johnson. 1986. Action research: Cooperative learning in the science classroom. *Science and Children* 24: 31–32.

Kagan, S. 1989. *The Structural Approach to Cooperative Learning.* Educational Leadership 47: 12–15.

Koda, K. 2007. Reading and language learning: Cross linguistic constraints on second language reading development. *Language Learning* 57(Suppl. 1): 1–44.

Krashen, S. D. 1982. *Principles and practice in second language acquisition.* Oxford: Pergamon.

Krashen, S. D. and T. D. Terrell. 2000. *The natural approach: Language acquisition in the classroom.* Edingburgh Gate, Harlow: Pearson Education Second Impression.

Lemke, J. L. 2002. Multimedia semiotics: Genres for science education and scientific literacy. In *Developing advanced literacy in first and second languages: Meaning with power*, eds. M. J. Schleppegrell and M. C. Colombi, 21–44. London: Lawrence Erlbaum Associates.

Lesaux, N. and E. Geva, 2006. Synthesis: Development of literacy in language-minority students. In *Developing literacy in second-language learners: Report of the National Literacy Panel on language-minority children and youth*, eds. D. August and T. Shanahan, 53–74. Mahwah, NJ: Lawrence Erlbaum Associates.

Malik, A. A. 1990. A psycholinguistic analysis of the reading behavior of EFL-proficient readers using culturally familiar and culturally nonfamiliar expository texts. *American Educational Research Journal* 27 (1): 205–23.

Marzano, R. J. 2004. *Building background knowledge for academic achievement: Research on what works in schools.* Alexandria, Virginia: Association for Supervision Development and Curriculum.

McNeil, J.D. 1992. *Reading comprehension: New directions for classroom practice*, 3rd. ed. Los Angeles: University of California.

National Center for Educational Statistics. 2006–2007. National assessment of educational progress: The nation's report card (NCES 2007496). Retrieved from http://nces.ed.gov/programs/stateprofiles/sresult.asp?mode=fullanddisplaycat=1ands1=48.

National Center for Educational Statistics. 2007. National assessment of educational progress: The nation's report card (NCES 2007496). Retrieved from http://nationsreportcard.gov/reading_2007/r0015.asp?subtab_id=Tab_2andtab_id=tab1#chart.

Ogle, D. M. 1986. K-W-L: A teaching model that develops active reading of expository text. *The Reading Teacher* 39 (6): 564–570.

Roe, B., S. H. Smith, and P. C. Burns. 2008. *Teaching reading in today's elementary schools*, 10th ed. Independence, KY: Cengage Learning.

References Cited (cont.)

• •

Scarcella, R. C. 2003. *Accelerating academic English: A focus on English language learners*. Oakland: Regents of the University of California.

Scarcella, R. C., E. S. Anderson, and S. D. Krashen. 1991. *Developing communicative competence in a second language: Issues in second language research*. New York: HarperCollins.

Schleppegrell, M. J., 2004. *The language of schooling: a functional linguistics perspective*. Mahwah, NJ: Lawrence Erlbaum Associates.

Schleppegrell, M. J., M. Achugar, and T. Oteíza. 2004. The grammar of history: Enhancing content-based instruction through a functional focus on language. *TESOL Quarterly* 38(1): 67–93.

Scieszka, Jon. *The True Story of the Three Little Pigs!* New York: Puffin, 1996.

Short, D. 1994. Expanding middle school horizons: Integrating language, culture, and social studies. *TESOL Quarterly* 28 (3): 581–608.

Slavin, R. E. 1989. Research on cooperative learning: An international perspective. *Scandinavian Journal of Educational Research* 33 (4): 231–243.

Spanos, G., N. C. Rhodes, T. C. Dale, and J. Crandall. 1988. Linguistic features of mathematical problem solving: Insights and applications. In *Linguistics and cultural influences on mathematics*, eds. R. R. Cocking and J.P. Mestre. 221–40. Hillsdale, NJ: Erlbaum.

Stubbs, M. 2008 Which words must students know? A note on "A New Academic Word List." Retrieved from University of Trier, Department of Linguistics. Retrieved from http://teacher.scholastic.com/products/read180/community/pdfs/Vocabulary/Academic_Word_List_by_Frequency.pdf

Swain, M. 1985. Communicative competence: Some roles of comprehensible input and comprehensible output in its development. In *Input in second language acquisition*, ed. S. M. Gass and C. G. Madden, 235–57. Rowley, MA: Newbury House Publishers.

U.S. Census Bureau. 2006. 2006 American community survey. Washington D.C. Retreived from http://www.census.gov/prod/2008pubs/p20-559.pdf-2008-09-17.

Wellington, J. and J. Osborne, 2001. *Language and literacy in science education*. Buckingham, England: Open University Press.

WIDA—housed within the Wisconsin center for Education Research. 2007. English language proficiency standards. The Board of Regents of the University of Wisconsin System, http://www.wida.us/standards/elp.aspx.

Wong-Fillmore, L. and C. Snow. 2000. What teachers need to know about language. In *What teachers need to know about language*, eds. C.T. Adger, C.E. Snow, and D. Christian, 7–43. Washington, D.C.: Center for Applied Linguistics.

Contents of the Teacher Resource CD

Page	Resource	Filename
Planning for Explicit Teaching		
34	Lesson Design Template	lessondesign.pdf
Schema and Vocabulary Building		
88	Cognates	cognates.pdf
90	Root Words	rootwords.pdf
95	Affixes	affixes.pdf
97	Academic Word Lists	academiclist.pdf
102	Circle Map	circlemap.pdf
103	K/W/H/L Chart	kwhlchart.pdf
104	Word Definition Map	worddefinition.pdf
105	Everyday to Specalized Content	everyday.pdf
Comprehensible Input		
122	Sentence Frames	sentence.pdf
125	Signal Words	signalwords.pdf
127	Graphic Organizer for Comparing and Contrasting	compare.pdf
128	Graphic Organizer for Cause and Effect	cause.pdf
129	Graphic Organizer for Classifying and Categorizing	classify.pdf
130	Graphic Organizer for Sequencing	sequence.pdf
131	Graphic Organizer for Main Ideas	mainidea.pdf
132	Graphic Organizer for Fact and Opinion	factopinion.pdf
Opportunities for Practice		
160	Think-Write-Pair-Share Journal	thinkwritepair.pdf
161	Talking Chips	talkchip.pdf
162	Not Taboo	nottaboo.pdf
163	Mix-Freeze-Match	mixfreezematch.pdf

Contents of the Teacher Resource CD *(cont.)*

Page	Resource	Filename
Opportunities for Practice *(cont.)*		
164	Give and Take	givetake.pdf
165	Clock Appointments	clock.pdf
166	Passing the Pen	passpen.pdf
Lesson Design		
191	Horizontal Lesson Design Template	horizontal.pdf

Notes

• • • • • • •

Notes

• • • • • • •